SUNDAY IS NOT THE
SABBATH?

Apostle Arthur Bailey, D. Div.

Published and produced in the United States of America by
Arthur Bailey Ministries, P O Box 49744, Charlotte, NC 28277

Copyright 2014 Arthur Bailey Ministries
P O Box 49744
Charlotte, NC 28277

ISBN 978-0-9833765-9-0
Library of Congress Control Number: 2014941249

All scripture is taken from the *King James Version* (KJV), the *New King James Version* (NKJV), or the *Complete Jewish Bible* (CJB).

In scripture quotations and in the text, words in **bold type** or in brackets, [ ], indicate that the emphasis was added by the author.

Edited by Sharon Campbell and PJ Langhoff

For more information visit, www.ArthurBaileyMinistries.com, or email ArthurBaileyMinistries@gmail.com

TABLE OF CONTENTS

Acknowledgment.. 4

Introduction 5

Chapter 1   The Search Begins............................... 13

Chapter 2:   Just the Scriptures.............................. 21

Chapter 3:   Origins of the Sabbath......................... 25

Chapter 4:   Facts About the Sabbath...................... 33

Chapter 5:   The LORD's Day 39

Chapter 6:   Frequently Asked Questions 45

Chapter 7:   Traditions of Men................................ 65

Chapter 8:   Observing the Sabbath 71

Chapter 9:   Scriptural Guidelines for the Sabbath 77

Chapter 10:   The Messiah in the Sabbath 95

Chapter 11:   Benefits of the Sabbath 97

Chapter 12:   How We Celebrate the Sabbath 105

Epilogue: Has It Been Worth it?........................... 109

Appendix A: Denominational Statements About

The Sabbath....................................... 119

Appendix B: Hebrew Names for Weekdays............ 141

Appendix C: Origins of Secular Weekday Names 143

About the Author.. 145

DVD Teachings by Arthur Bailey............................ 147

I find myself in debt to The Baptists, Pentecostals, Charismatics, Missouri Synod Lutherans and The Christian Reformed Church of North America, all who have played a major role; and various other denominations who have played minor roles, but were totally unaware they were helping to bring forth this book.

I thank my wife Marvina who has navigated these troubled, religious, denominational waters with me; searching for truth and knowing that I had no idea where I was going, but knowing beyond a doubt who I was following.

I am very thankful for the congregations that supported me, and the individuals who stood with me along this journey in search of the True Gospel of the Kingdom, and The Messiah who gave His life for us to have this faith once delivered to the saints.

Thank you to all who read this book and apply the truths revealed within these pages. May you fully enjoy this life Yeshua came to give!

Shalom! Shabbat Shalom!

INTRODUCTION

These were more noble than those in Thessalonica, in that they received the word with all readiness of mind, and searched the scriptures daily, whether those things were so.
Acts 17:11, KJV

The Sabbath is one of the most important subjects in scripture. The Fourth Commandment calls for a Sabbath on the seventh day of the week. Unfortunately the Sabbath is the commandment most ignored by the majority of those who confess faith in Yeshua the Messiah (Jesus). Theologians, preachers and teachers have been teaching that God, the apostles, or the early church Fathers changed the seventh-day Sabbath to be on Sunday in honor of the resurrection of the Messiah.

There is no biblical evidence to support such teaching. Many scriptures that are used to support this argument have no reference supporting a change of Sabbath. The Roman Catholic Church implemented this change and still takes credit for it, and I shall explain this change a bit later.

As a product of a Sunday service denominational church; for most of my life I have taught, defended, and justified the Sunday Sabbath doctrine. However, through diligent study of His Word, YeHoVaH (God's Hebrew name) has shown me that this teaching was in error. Neither He nor the apostles ever changed the seventh-day Sabbath to be held as Sunday worship.

In January 2004, I invited my apostolic oversight churches to participate in a seven-day complete fast, with variations for those unable to do a total fast. We were seeking direction for our local church, Abundant Life International Ministries; and the Kenyan and Philippine churches. Immediately after the fast, YeHoVaH asked me, "Why do you worship on Sunday?"

God had never asked me this question before! However, I had answered this question many times with a well-prepared religious answer that was sufficient for me and for anyone who did not understand scripture.

After careful meditation, I responded with a traditional religious answer, "Because I have always worshipped on Sunday. That's what I was taught to do."

When YeHoVaH challenged me with this question, I was shocked and ashamed at my response as a preacher. I of all people, "Mr. Anti-Traditional-to-the-core," was operating from tradition and nullifying the Word of God concerning the Sabbath.

Growing up, my parents took me to church every Sunday and to occasional weekday revival meetings. Every practicing Christian I knew attended church on Sunday for worship services. The only exceptions were the Seventh-day Adventists who held their services on the Sabbath. However, they were labeled as a legalistic cult that depended upon strict adherence to parts of the Law/Torah for their salvation. This practice was clearly contrary to scripture; according to my denominational teaching.

Like most people, I had been taught that Sunday had taken the place of the Sabbath mentioned in the Fourth Commandment because the Messiah was resurrected on Sunday. I had accepted this doctrine at face value without thoroughly understanding the Word.

As a result of studying His Word, and laying the denominational traditions aside, I have come to understand the seventh-day Sabbath as the day of rest and worship.

According to scriptures, YeHoVaH declared this as a day to rest and to hold a holy convocation. The Sabbath is a gift from God to man.

> ***Leviticus 23:3***, *"Six days shall work be done: but the seventh day is the sabbath of rest, an holy convocation; ye shall do no work therein: it is the sabbath of the LORD in all your dwellings." KJV*

Yeshua clearly stated that He did not come to abolish or to destroy the Law/Torah; but to fulfill it. The word "fulfill" in this case means "to meet the requirements of," "to satisfy," or "to put into effect." Yeshua said:

> ***Matthew 5:17-20***, *"Think not that I am come to destroy the law [Torah] or the prophets: I am not come to destroy, but to fulfill. For verily I say unto you, till heaven and earth pass, one jot or one tittle shall in no wise pass from the law [Torah], till all be fulfilled. Whosoever therefore shall break one of these least commandments, and shall teach men so, he shall be called the least in the kingdom of heaven: but whosoever shall do and teach them, the same shall be called great in the kingdom of heaven. For I say unto you, that except your righteousness shall exceed the righteousness of the scribes and Pharisees, ye shall in no case enter into the kingdom of heaven." KJV*

Major fears exist among believers of denominational doctrines concerning issues of the Law/Torah, legalism, control, and bondage. Much of this fear is related to Pharisaic teachings, which ultimately became known and referred to by the Messiah as the "commandments of men."

Matthew 15:9, *"But in vain they do worship me, teaching for doctrines the commandments of men." KJV*

Yeshua declared that the commandments of men made the Commandments of YeHoVaH ineffective.

Matthew 15:6, *"Thus have ye made the commandment of God of none effect by your tradition." KJV*

We must realize that Satan has been opposing the truth from the beginning. He uses anything and everything he can to deter people from following the truth. Man has exalted the laws of men (traditions) above the Law/Torah of YeHoVaH. Man uses scriptures to justify compliance to traditions while simultaneously desecrating the Law/Torah and the Commandments of YeHoVaH.

One is viewed as a rebel and sinner for disregarding man-made laws like exceeding the speed limit or failing to wear a safety belt. Christians use *Romans 13* as a divine endorsement for obeying the law of the land; while out of the same mouth they emphatically state that we are no longer under God's Law/Torah.

Romans 13:1-2, *"Let every soul be subject unto the higher powers. For there is no power but of God: the powers that be are ordained of God. Whosoever therefore resisteth the power resisteth the ordinance of God: and they that resist shall receive to themselves damnation." KJV*

Yeshua tied the Commandments to salvation when He said:

John 14:15, *"If ye love me, keep my commandments." KJV*

Furthermore, Paul wrote:

8

Romans 7:12, "wherefore the law [Torah] is holy, and the Commandment holy, and just, and good." KJV

This book in no way advocates Judaism, Seventh-day Adventist, or any other denominational doctrinal belief. However it is an honest, sincere effort to look at scripture simply as scripture. I wish to bring understanding to what the Bible has to say about the Fourth Commandment, which is also called the seventh-day Sabbath.

Throughout this book I will use some terms that are a little different from mainline Christian teachings. They are:

- *The word **'god'** impersonally refers to The Creator (Exodus 20:1-2), idols (Exodus 20:3), and men (Psalms 82:6), with upper and lower case variations.*

- ***YeHoVaH** is God's Hebrew name.*

- ***Yeshua** is the name the angel spoke to Mary to give to her Son. It is a Jewish name for a Jewish boy, who was, and is the Son of the Most High Elohim. The name "Jesus" is a transliteration of the Latin word "Iesus" (Hay-soos); which is a transliteration of the Greek word "Iesous" (Yesus). This name is supposedly translated from the Hebrew name "Yeshua."*

- ***Elohim/elohim** is the Hebrew name for God/god.*

- ***Shalom** means peace, tranquility, safety, well-being, welfare, health contentment, success, comfort, wholeness, and integrity.*

- ***Torah** means teaching, Law, the Five Books of Moses, and the Pentateuch.*

- ***Messianic** pertains to Yeshua the Messiah; a person who keeps the Law/Torah and has faith in Yeshua.*

- **Hebrew Roots** *refers to returning to observing the Law/Torah which was given to the Hebrew people for all the nations.*

> **Man has exalted the laws of man above the Law of God.**

Within this book I address key New Testament scriptures that have been used to support the changing of the Sabbath from the seventh day to the first day of the week. Chapter Six is devoted to the most critical and the most common questions and arguments used in Christian denominational debates when addressing the Sabbath Commandment and the Law/Torah such as:

- *Didn't Yeshua come to destroy the keeping of the Law/Torah?*
- *Can I choose any day to be my Sabbath?*
- *Wasn't the Sabbath changed from Saturday to Sunday because Yeshua arose from the grave on the first day of the week?*
- *Did Paul keep the Sabbath on Sunday?*

> **Yehovah asked me this question: "Why do you worship on Sunday?"**

The Holy Spirit has compelled me to share the profound revelation I have received through my studies. It is my prayer that when you read the following pages, you will allow the Holy Spirit to show you whether or not these things that are written are true. YeHoVaH has spoken through His Son in His Word:

> **John 8:32**, *"And ye shall know the truth, and the truth shall make you free."* KJV

My goal for writing this book is to inspire you to search the scriptures for yourself. The challenge for you will be to cast off religious or traditional mindsets and to seek His Truth and His Face.

Throughout this book I expose the deceptions and strong delusions of religious traditions that have led the Christian Church in the wrong direction for hundreds of years. I hope you will choose to disconnect from

"On the venerable Day of the Sun let the magistrates and people residing in cities rest, and let all workshops be closed."
Constantine's decree,
March 7, 321 A.D.

the paganized religious system called the Corporate American Church; and be able to connect to the one true Elohim, YeHoVaH. Once you have discovered the hidden truths of scripture, you will understand **why we should observe the seventh-day Sabbath as the proper day of rest and worship.**

May the blessings of the Most High be with you as we embark together on this journey through the scriptures in the name that is above every other name, YESHUA!

Shalom,

Apostle Arthur Bailey

Chapter One

THE SEARCH BEGINS

Let us therefore no longer keep the Sabbath after the Jewish manner, and rejoice in the days of idleness; for "he that does not work, let him not eat. . . . let every friend of Christ keep the Lord's day as a festival, the resurrection day, the queen and chief of all the days [of the week]"
Ignatius, 107 A.D.

For over seventeen hundred years, the Christian Church believed and followed a lie that was first conjured up during the second century, and made law by Constantine the Great during the third century. Man asserted that God or the apostles changed the day of worship from Sabbath on the seventh day of the week, to Sunday; the first day of the week.

Much of the material supporting this change came from the Protestant Christian or Catholic point of view. It also centers on the writings of the early church Fathers; not the apostles of scripture. Many of these early church Fathers were non-Hebrews, anti-Semitic and from Roman Catholic backgrounds. They interpreted the scriptures from a Western cultural perspective.

Observance of Sunday as the primary day of worship appears to have solidified during the reign of Emperor Hadrian (A.D. 117-135); who harshly persecuted Hebrews throughout the Roman Empire. Hadrian specifically prohibited practices of Judaism, including observance of the seventh-day Sabbath.

These oppressive measures apparently influenced many early Christians in Rome to abandon the seventh day Sabbath and turn to Sunday. This day was historically observed by the Romans as a day of veneration of the sun. Within a few centuries, Sabbath observance by Christians was virtually eliminated within the confines of the empire and replaced by Sunday worship.

In order to fully understand the teachings in this book, you must understand these six basic interpretation rules; which are the premise for our discussion.

Rule 1

During the time of Yeshua's life on earth, there were NO New Testament writings. Only the Old Testament (Tanakh) existed. Yeshua and the apostles taught from the Tanakh. Biblical scholars disagree on the dates that the New Testament scriptures were written. However, the dates range from 40-125 AD. The Gospel writings, the Acts of the Apostles, the Pauline Letters, and the other New Testament writings, were written during and concerning the time when only the Old Testament existed.

Messiah Yeshua did not come to break, abolish, destroy, or void the Law/Torah, or the prophets.

> **Matthew 5:17-19**, *"Think not that I am come to destroy the law [Torah] or the prophets: I am not come to destroy, but to fulfil. For verily I say unto you, Till heaven and earth pass, one jot or one tittle shall in no wise pass from the law [Torah], till all be fulfilled. Whosoever therefore shall break one of these least commandments, and shall teach men so, he shall be called the least in the kingdom of heaven: but whosoever shall do and teach them, the same shall be called great in the kingdom of heaven." KJV*

Instead, **Yeshua taught from the Law/Torah, the Prophets, and the Writings or Tanakh (Old Testament).**

Luke 24:25-32, *"Then he said unto them, 'O fools, and slow of heart to believe all that the prophets have spoken: Ought not Christ [Messiah] to have suffered these things, and to enter into his glory?' And beginning at Moses and all the prophets, he expounded unto them in all the scriptures the things concerning himself. And they drew nigh unto the village, whither they went: and he made as though he would have gone further. But they constrained him, saying, 'Abide with us: for it is toward evening, and the day is far spent.' And he went in to tarry with them. And it came to pass, as he sat at meat with them, he took bread, and blessed it, and brake, and gave to them. And their eyes were opened, and they knew him; and he vanished out of their sight. And they said one to another, 'Did not our heart burn within us, while he talked with us by the way, and while he opened to us the scriptures?'" KJV*

After His resurrection, Yeshua told His disciples to teach others what He taught them.

Matthew 28:19-20, *"Go ye therefore, and teach all nations, baptizing them in the name of the Father, and of the Son, and of the Holy Ghost: Teaching them to observe all things whatsoever I have commanded you: and, lo, I am with you always, even unto the end of the world. Amen." KJV*

Rule 2

In many cities and towns, where **Gentiles** were being saved, they **were taught from the Tanakh (Old Testament).**

Acts 15:20-21, *"But that we write unto them, that they abstain from pollutions of idols, and from fornication, and from things strangled, and from blood. For Moses of old time hath in every city them that preach him, being read in the synagogues every sabbath day." KJV*

15

Rule 3

You must remember that Paul taught scripture, but he wrote letters answering questions and addressing the needs of different congregations as well as individuals. **Paul did not consider his letters as scripture** but as letters instructing new believers how to conduct themselves according to the scriptures. His letter to Timothy states:

> **2 Timothy 3:16**, *"All scripture is given by inspiration of God, and is profitable for doctrine, for reproof, for correction, for instructions in righteousness:"* KJV

What scripture was Paul talking about when the New Testament had not yet been written or adopted? **Every reference to the words "scripture" or "scriptures" in the Bible refers to the Old Testament.**

Rule 4

You must remember that **in the New Testament, the followers of Yeshua Messiah were familiar with the Tanakh (Old Testament) because that was what they were taught** when they went into the synagogues.

Rule 5

The Biblical revival in the book of Acts on the Day of Pentecost (a Feast of YeHoVaH), resulted in 3,000 Law/Torah observant men being saved. **This occurred before the books of Matthew, Mark, Luke and John were written; nor were there any writings of Paul**. In *Acts 4*, the number of saved observers grew to 5,000 men. By chapter 21, there were many more thousands who were all zealous for the Law/Torah. The Darby Bible uses the word "myriads," which the Greek translates to tens of thousands.

Acts 21:20, " On hearing it, they praised God; but they also said to him, 'You see, brother, how many tens of thousands of believers there are among the Judeans, and they are all zealots for the Torah [Law].'" CJB

Rule 6

You must remember that **the Bible was written in the Middle-Eastern cultural context** by predominantly Hebrew people as the Holy Spirit inspired them. The culture was Middle-Eastern, and so were the customs. Westerners tend to misconstrue the gist of some of the biblical accounts. They interpret the Scriptures with a Western mindset according to their own cultural tenets.

The application of these six rules will greatly enhance our understanding of the New Testament letters that Paul wrote to the various individuals and congregations. They will also assist with our understanding of the writings of the Gospels; the Acts of the Apostles, Hebrews, James, Peter, John, Jude, and Revelation.

Having laid the ground rules to aid in the comprehension of this writing; let us proceed to the heart of the matter, which is that **Sunday Is Not The Sabbath.**

The subject of the seventh-day Sabbath is probably one of the most important subjects contained in the Holy Scriptures, and yet it is the least observed among Christians. Of the Ten

This book is not influenced by Orthodox Judaism or Seventh-day Adventism.

Commandments, it is the only Commandment YeHoVaH told His people to **REMEMBER.** It is also the only commandment that not only is not being observed; it has also been utterly forgotten. **REMEMBER** implies that observance was a concept the people were fully conversant with **before the giving of the Law/Torah on Mount Sinai** in *Exodus 20.*

> *Exodus 16:23-26, "And he said unto them, 'This is that which the LORD hath said; To morrow is the rest of the holy sabbath unto the LORD: bake that which ye will bake to day, and seethe that ye will seethe; and that which remaineth over lay up for you to be kept until the morning.' And they laid it up till the morning, as Moses bade: and it did not stink, neither was there any worm therein. And Moses said, 'eat that to day; for to day is a sabbath unto the LORD: to day ye shall not find it in the field. Six days ye shall gather it; but on the seventh day, which is the sabbath, in it there shall be none.'" KJV*

Why must we have another book about the Sabbath? Most of the books about this subject were written by Orthodox Jews who had not accepted Yeshua, the Son of YeHoVaH; or by Seventh-day Adventist scholars. The Christian Church will accept neither of these religious groups' writings.

Remember the sabbath day, to keep it holy.
Exodus 20:8, KJV

Christian authors on the subject of the Sabbath assume that Sunday is the Sabbath; which is an assumption unsupported by scripture. The Encyclopedia Britannica states in the History of the Church Year about Sunday that: "Regular Christian corporate worship on Sundays goes back to the apostolic age, but New Testament writings do not explain how the practice began."

I have received the revelation of the seventh-day Sabbath from YeHoVaH Himself. Again, this book is not influenced by any form of Judaism or Seventh-day Adventism, but is the result of my personal in-depth study of YeHoVaH's Word, and other sources mentioned in this writing as the Holy Spirit has inspired.

I believe that the reader's eyes will be opened as mine have been. It will be easy to see how we have been tricked by the devil and by traditional religious practices to abandon the Sabbath and to embrace a pagan day of worship on Sun-Day (Day of the Sun – Webster). The observance of this day is clearly a major violation of YeHoVaH's Fourth Commandment.

The Sun-day worship has nothing to do with Christianity, and everything to do with ancient religions. The ancient Greeks felt that the sun was the source of life on the planet, and gave it prime importance in their thinking. When the Romans later adopted the seven-day week, they emphasized their respect for the sun by naming the first day of the week as *"dies solis,"* or "day of the sun." According to the Encyclopedia Mythica, "sun's day" is the name of a pagan Roman holiday. It is also called "Dominica" (Latin), or "the Day of God."

"Knowing this first, that no prophecy of the scripture is of any private interpretation. For the prophecy came not in old time by the will of man: but holy men of God spake as they were moved by the Holy Ghost."
2 Peter 1:20-21, KJV

Solomon, the wisest man ever to live (*I Kings 3: 12*), shared some of his most precious wisdom with us when he said:

> *Ecclesiastes 12:12-14, "And further, by these, my son, be admonished: of making many books there is no end; and much study is a weariness of the flesh. Let us hear the conclusion of the whole matter: Fear God, and keep his commandments: for this is the whole duty of man. For God shall bring every work into judgment, with every secret thing, whether it be good, or whether it be evil." KJV*

The following scriptures are additional words of wisdom for those who strive for righteous conduct by keeping YeHoVaH's Commandments. These scriptures will also serve as a foundation for the remainder of this book. Please keep an open mind as we search the scriptures together.

> *Genesis 2:3, "And God blessed the seventh day, and sanctified it: because that in it he had rested from all his work which God created and made." KJV*

> *Exodus 20:8-11, "Remember the sabbath day, to keep it holy. Six days shalt thou labour, and do all thy work: But the seventh day is the sabbath of the LORD thy God: in it thou shalt not do any work, thou, nor thy son, nor thy daughter, thy manservant, nor thy maidservant, nor thy cattle, nor thy stranger that is within thy gates: For in six days the LORD made heaven and earth, the sea, and all that in them is, and*

rested the seventh day: wherefore the LORD blessed the sabbath day, and hallowed it." KJV

Matthew 5:17-19, "Think not that I am come to destroy the law [Torah] or the prophets: I am not come to destroy, but to fulfill. For verily I say unto you, till heaven and earth pass, one jot or one tittle shall in no wise pass from the law [Torah], till all be fulfilled. Whosoever therefore shall break one of these least commandments, and shall teach men so, he shall be called the least in the kingdom of heaven: but whosoever shall do and teach them, the same shall be called great in the kingdom of heaven." KJV

John 14:15, "If ye love me, keep my commandments." KJV

John 14:21, "He that hath my commandments, and keepeth them, he it is that loveth me: and he that loveth me shall be loved of my Father, and I will love him, and will manifest myself to him." KJV

John 15:10, "If ye keep my commandments, ye shall abide in my love; even as I have kept my **The scriptures are clear in that the seventh-day Sabbath is a binding Commandment.** *Father's commandments, and abide in his love." KJV*

1 John 2:3, "And hereby we do know that we know him, if we keep his commandments." KJV

1 John 2:4, "He that saith, I know him, and keepeth not his commandments, is a liar, and the truth is not in him." KJV

1 John 3:22, "And whatsoever we ask, we receive of him, because we keep his commandments, and do those things that are pleasing in his sight." KJV

1 John 3:24, "And he that keepeth his commandments dwelleth in him, and he in him. And hereby we know that he abideth in us, by the Spirit which he hath given us." KJV

1 John 5:2-3, "By this we know that we love the children of God, when we love God, and keep his commandments. For this is the love of God, that we keep his commandments: and his commandments are not grievous." KJV

2 John 1:6, *"And this is love that we walk after his commandments. This is the commandment, that, as ye have heard from the beginning, ye should walk in it." KJV*

Revelation 12:17, *"The dragon was infuriated over the woman and went off to fight the rest of her children, those who obey God's commands and bear witness to Yeshua." CJB*

Revelation 14:12, *"Here is the patience of the saints: here are they that keep the commandments of God, and the faith of Jesus [Yeshua]." KJV*

> **"Sabbath is a part of the Decalogue – the Ten Commandments. This alone forever settles the question as to the perpetuity of the institution…Until, therefore, it can be shown that the whole moral law has been repealed, the Sabbath will stand…The teaching of Christ confirms the perpetuity of the Sabbath."**
> T.C. Blake, D.D.

Chapter Three

ORIGINS OF THE SABBATH

"The Sabbath was binding in Eden, and it has been in force ever since. This fourth commandment begins with the word 'remember,' showing that the Sabbath already existed when God wrote the law on the tables of stone at Sinai. How can men claim that this one commandment has been done away with when they will admit that the other nine are still binding?"
D.L. Moody

Whenever the conversation arises concerning the Sabbath, well-meaning believers find a verse or two from the gospels and Paul's letters to support a doctrine that insists that the Sabbath was changed from the seventh to the first day of the week. This changed day is commonly referred to as "The Lord's Day."

This concept is extracted from *Revelation 1:10*. However this scripture is not a clear defense for such doctrine because it requires some private, personal, or denominational interpretation to bridge the gap between the verse and the alteration of the Sabbath to Sunday.

Revelation 1:10, *"I was in the Spirit on the Lord's Day, and heard behind me a great voice, as of a trumpet."* KJV

The Scriptures however, are very clear concerning the origin of the Sabbath; and by whom it was established.

Genesis 2:3, *"And God blessed the seventh day, and sanctified it: because that in it he had rested from all his work which God created and made."* KJV

Exodus 20:10a, *"But the seventh day is the sabbath of the LORD thy God:"* KJV

The Scriptures also clearly state that the Sabbath is the seventh day of the week.

> ***Exodus 20:9-10a****, "Six days shalt thou labour, and do all thy work: But the seventh day is the sabbath of the LORD thy God:" KJV*

The Scriptures are keenly clear that the Sabbath is a Commandment from God, and part of the Ten Commandments.

> ***Exodus 20:8-11****, "Remember the sabbath day, to keep it holy. Six days shalt thou labour, and do all thy work: But the seventh day is the sabbath of the LORD thy God: in it thou shalt not do any work, thou, nor thy son, nor thy daughter, thy manservant, nor thy maidservant, nor thy cattle, nor thy stranger that is within thy gates: For in six days the LORD made heaven and earth, the sea, and all that in them is, and rested the seventh day: wherefore the LORD blessed the sabbath day, and hallowed it." KJV*

The Scriptures are extraordinarily clear that the Commandments of God were written by the finger of God Himself, and given to Moses. They are not the Law/Torah of Moses, or the Commandments of Moses, but the Commandments of God.

> ***Exodus 31:18****, "And he gave unto Moses, when he had made an end of communing with him upon Mount Sinai, two tables of testimony, tables of stone, written with the finger of God." KJV*

The Scriptures are also clear that Yeshua honored the Sabbath; and so did Paul and the early Messianic Communities.

Yeshua honored the Sabbath.

Luke 4:16, "So He came to Nazareth, where He had been brought up. And as His custom was, He went into the synagogue on the Sabbath day, and stood up to read." NKJV

Paul honored the Sabbath.

Acts 13:13-14, "Now when Paul and his party set sail from Paphos, they came to Perga in Pamphylia; and John, departing from them, returned to Jerusalem. But when they departed from Perga, they came to Antioch in Pisidia, and went into the synagogue on the Sabbath day and sat down." NKJV

The Sabbath is the seventh day of the week, or Saturday; which God set aside.

Acts 17:2, "Then Paul, as his custom was, went in to them, and for three Sabbaths reasoned with them from the Scriptures..." NKJV

Acts 18:4, "and he reasoned in the synagogue every sabbath, and persuaded the Jews and the Greeks." KJV

The early Messianic Communities honored the Sabbath.

Acts 13:42-44, "As Paul and Barnabas were leaving the synagogue, the people invited them to speak further about these things on the next Sabbath. On the next Sabbath almost the whole city gathered to hear the word of the Lord." KJV

These were Jews and Gentiles honoring the Sabbath (*Acts 13:44-48*). If Sunday was the Lord's Day of worship, why did they not meet the following day? Why would they wait until the next Sabbath to hear Paul speak?

Our Heavenly Father gave us the Sabbath as a sign between Himself and His children.

Another instance of Paul keeping the Sabbath is illustrated in Acts.

Acts 16:13-15, "And on the Sabbath day we went out of the city to the riverside, where prayer was customarily made; and we sat down and spoke to the women who met there. Now a certain woman named Lydia heard us. She was a seller of purple from the city of Thyatira, who worshiped God. The Lord opened her heart to heed the things spoken by Paul. And when she and her household were baptized, she begged us, saying, 'If you have judged me to be faithful to the Lord, come to my house and stay.' So she persuaded us." NKJV

From the above scriptures we can clearly conclude that:

- *The Scriptures are clear concerning the origins of the Sabbath and the authority behind its endorsement.*

- *The seventh day of the week was, and still is designated as the Sabbath day.*

- *Keeping the Sabbath is a Commandment of God and part of the Ten Commandments.*

- *The Scriptures clearly state that the Commandments of God were written by the finger of God and given to Moses.*

- *The Commandments are not the Law/Torah of Moses or the Commandments of Moses, but the Commandments of God.*

The Sabbath Commandment was so vital to God's people, that violating it warranted a death penalty:

Exodus 35:1-2, "Then Moses gathered all the congregation of the children of Israel together, and said to them, 'These are the words which the LORD has commanded you to do: Work shall be done for six days, but the seventh day shall be a holy day for you, a Sabbath of rest to the LORD. Whoever does any work on it shall be put to death.'" NKJV

28

In Numbers, we find the Israelite assembly enforcing the death penalty for violating the Sabbath:

Numbers 15:32-36, "And while the children of Israel were in the wilderness, they found a man that gathered sticks upon the sabbath day. And they that found him gathering sticks brought him unto Moses and Aaron, and unto all the congregation. And they put him in ward, because it was not declared what should be done to him. And the LORD said unto Moses, 'The man shall be surely put to death: all the congregation shall stone him with stones without the camp.' And all the congregation brought him without the camp, and stoned him with stones, and he died; as the LORD commanded Moses." KJV

Once my eyes were opened, I was amazed at the level and depth of the "traditions of man" in which I had operated. For years I had read over the scriptures and become complacent without fully understanding certain passages. Thus, a lack of diligence in seeking God for the truth led to the acceptance of denominational religious traditions.

Mark 7:6-9, "'...This people honoureth me with their lips, but their heart is far from me. Howbeit in vain do they worship me, teaching for doctrines the commandments of men. For laying aside the commandment of God, ye hold the tradition of men, as the washing of pots and cups: and many other such like things ye do.' And he said unto them, 'Full well ye reject the commandment of God, that ye may keep your own tradition.'" KJV

The majority of preachers manipulate the Old Testament writings to their advantage. In the most illustrious manner they extract what they want, and reject the rest. Contemporary religious leaders use the Old Testament to control New Testament believers; while from the pulpit they conveniently reject its authority. For example, tithing is an Old Testament teaching. However, almost every preacher and church has adopted the practice of tithing.

The coveted blessings mentioned in *Deuteronomy 28* depend upon the condition stipulated within the first two verses; which very few believers ever acknowledge.

> *Deuteronomy 28:1-2*, *"If you fully obey the LORD your God and carefully follow all his commands I give you today, the LORD your God will set you high above all the nations on earth. All these blessings will come upon you and accompany you if you obey the LORD your God."* KJV

The prophet Hosea bemoans the imminent demise of Israel for ignoring the Law/Torah of God:

> *Hosea 4:6*, *"My people are destroyed for lack of knowledge. Because you have rejected knowledge, I also will reject you from being priest for Me; Because you have forgotten the law [Torah] of your God, I also will forget your children."* NKJV

How often do we hear preachers wailing from the pulpit how YeHoVaH's people are destroyed for lack of knowledge! Yet very few ever mention the rest of the verse. Being rejected by YeHoVaH is the direct consequence of rejecting the knowledge of the Law/Torah. This penalty spans generations. When you ignore His Law/Torah, YeHoVaH ignores your children.

The seventh day is a Sabbath of rest; a day of sacred assembly.

A similar judgment befell Saul when he failed to honor God's command. This led to the rejection of Saul as king.

1 Samuel 2:30, *"...for them that honour me I will honour, and they that despise me shall be lightly esteemed." KJV*

This knowledge of God's Law/Torah is being made available to you now. Will you be like the people of Hosea's day that rejected His knowledge; or will you be like the Bereans of Paul's day?

Acts 17:11, *"These were more noble than those in Thessalonica, in that they received the word with all readiness of mind, and searched the scriptures daily, whether those things were so." KJV*

"The observance of the Sabbath is fundamental to our argument in support of the origins of man and all creation... Yahweh is a God of truth. Our neglect of this law means that we agree with Darwinism and the big bang theory. We may just as well join them."
Albert Smith
Catholic Chancellor of the Archdiocese of Baltimore

The word "Sabbath" (*Shabbat* in Hebrew; *Sabbaton* in Greek) means to "desist," "cease," or "rest." Observing the Sabbath was first modeled by our Heavenly Father as a pattern for us to follow. This was done long before He gave the Law/Torah to Moses on Mount Sinai.

> *Genesis 2:1-3*, *"Thus the heavens and the earth were finished, and all the host of them. And on the seventh day God ended his work which he had made; and he rested on the seventh day from all his work, which he had made. And God blessed the seventh day, and sanctified it: because that in it he had rested from all his work which God created and made." KJV*

Please note what God said to Moses in *Exodus 16* before He gave the Ten Commandments in *Exodus 20*.

> *Exodus 16:28*, *"And the LORD said unto Moses, How long refuse ye to keep my commandments and my laws [Torah]?" KJV*

This is further evidence that the Sabbath was instituted at creation for all mankind.

Throughout the Scriptures, Sabbath is indicated for all people who join themselves to Israel by keeping the covenant (Commandments) of YeHoVaH.

> *Isaiah 56:2-7*, *"Blessed is the man that doeth this, and the son of man that layeth hold on it; that keepeth the sabbath from polluting it, and keepeth his hand from doing any evil. Neither let the son of the stranger, that hath joined himself to the*

LORD, speak, saying, The LORD hath utterly separated me from his people: neither let the eunuch say, Behold, I am a dry tree. For thus saith the LORD unto the eunuchs that keep my sabbaths, and choose the things that please me, and take hold of my covenant; Even unto them will I give in mine house and

Only the seventh day was blessed and set apart by the Creator.

within my walls a place and a name better than of sons and of daughters: I will give them an everlasting name, that shall not be cut off. Also the sons of the stranger, that join themselves to the LORD, to serve him, and to love the name of the LORD, to be his servants, ***every one that keepeth the sabbath from polluting it, and taketh hold of my covenant; Even them will I bring to my holy mountain, and make them joyful in my house of prayer:*** *their burnt offerings and their sacrifices shall be accepted upon mine altar; for mine house shall be called an house of prayer* ***for all people.***" *KJV*

As we proceed, keep in mind:

- *The Sabbath is the seventh day of the week, or Saturday; and not the first day, which is Sunday.*

- *God rested on the seventh day, and not any other day. God blessed the seventh day; He did not bless any other day he created.*

- *God sanctified the seventh day and set it apart from the other days.*

- *We should follow God's example to set apart the seventh day.*

- *The Sabbath originated at the end of creation (Genesis 2:1-3), and was reaffirmed in the Law/Torah in Exodus 20:8.*

Sabbath is the seventh day of the week, Saturday; which God set aside. We should also understand that God counts a day from evening to evening.

Genesis 1:5, *"God called the light Day, and the darkness he called Night. And the evening and the morning were the first day." KJV*

Leviticus 23:32b, *"from even unto even, shall ye celebrate your sabbath." [from sunset to sunset] KJV*

Our Heavenly Father gave us the Sabbath as a sign between Himself and His children. **The Sabbath is a perpetual covenant. It has no end!**

Exodus 31:16-18, *"Wherefore the children of Israel shall keep the sabbath, to observe the sabbath throughout their generations, for a perpetual covenant. It is a sign between me and the children of Israel forever: for in six days the LORD made heaven and earth, and on the seventh day he rested, and was refreshed. And he gave unto Moses, when he had made an end of communing with him upon Mount Sinai, two tables of testimony, tables of stone, written with the finger of God." KJV*

God used the Sabbath to test the children of Israel to see if they would walk in His Law/Torah or not. According to the passage below, if we fail this test by not observing the Sabbath, then we will not keep the rest of God's commands.

Exodus 16:4, *"The LORD said to Moses, I will rain down bread from heaven for you. The people are to go out each day and gather enough for that day. In this way I will test them and see whether they will follow my instructions. On the sixth day they are to prepare what they bring in, and that is to be twice as much as they gather on the other days." KJV*

In *Exodus 16:15-28*, God gave instruction to Moses concerning the gathering of the manna. On the sixth day the people were to gather twice as much as the other days.

However, instead of the leftovers breeding worms on the seventh day (as it would have on other days), God blessed the bread that the people might eat it without working on the seventh day. Some of the people from the congregation did not follow Moses' instructions. They went out to gather manna on the seventh day and found none.

> ***Exodus 16:29-30****, "See, for that the LORD hath given you the sabbath, therefore he giveth you on the sixth day the bread of two days; abide ye every man in his place, let no man go out of his place on the seventh day. So the people rested on the seventh day." KJV*

This verse also reiterates that the Sabbath is a gift of rest from God to man. Many will try to use this verse to say that we should not leave the home or go out of our place on the Sabbath; but

> *I John 3:4, defines sin as lawlessness.*

that is incorrect, as you will see later. A key to remember is that we have to look at scripture as a whole, and not at just one verse to determine or establish doctrine.

The Fourth Commandment concerning the Sabbath day is, and always has been the real "test" commandment (*cf. Exodus 16:4*). Many can accept the other nine: don't worship other gods, honor your parents, don't murder, etc., but the Fourth Commandment is different. Keeping it means visibly living quite differently from the society around you; and perhaps even being seen as peculiar.

As the Lord said to Moses,

> ***Exodus 19:5****, "Now therefore, if ye will obey my voice indeed, and keep my covenant, then ye shall be a **peculiar treasure** unto me above all people: for all the earth is mine:" KJV*

The Apostle Peter wrote,

> **1Peter 2:9**, *"But ye are a chosen generation, a royal priesthood, an holy nation, a **peculiar people**; that ye should show forth the praises of him who hath called you out of darkness into his marvelous light:" KJV*

Do you have the **Faith** and the **Courage** to obey God's Commandments even if it costs you everything including family and friends or your job? These are the challenges that most people have with obeying the Sabbath Commandment.

The Sabbath is a sign between Yehovah and the children of Israel forever.
From Exodus 31:17

Chapter Five

THE LORD'S DAY

"The observance of the Lord's Day (Sunday) is not founded on any command of God."
Augsburg Confession of Faith (Lutheran Church)

I have heard people say that Saturday is the Jewish Sabbath and that Sunday is the Christian Sabbath. There are no biblical or historical documents to support this doctrine or theory. The Law/Torah (the first five books of the Bible) which includes the Sabbath, was given on Mount Sinai. This is the same Law/Torah that is to be observed by Jews and Christians alike. The Jews call the first five books the **Law/Torah,** while Christians call them the **Pentateuch.** One term can be exchanged for the other.

Those who keep the Sunday "Sabbath" claim to be observing the Lord's Day. The term, "The Lord's Day" (in Greek, Kuriakos hemera, or "day belonging to the Lord") appears in scripture only in the Book of Revelation.

Revelation 1:10, "I was in the Spirit on the Lord's day, and heard behind me a great voice, as of a trumpet." KJV

Apostle John; the disciple Yeshua loved, wrote the Book of Revelation. He was also present when Yeshua declared:

Matthew 12:8, "For the Son of man is Lord even of the sabbath day." KJV

This statement concurs with the understanding that the Lord has always had a specific day from the beginning of time.

Exodus 20:10, "But the seventh day is the sabbath of the LORD thy God:" KJV

"Of" in this verse denotes the possessive case. He is the Lord who gave us the Sabbath.

Ezekiel 20:12, "Moreover also I gave them my sabbaths, to be a sign between me and them, that they might know that I am the LORD that sanctify them." KJV

Jeremiah 31:33 states that in the new Covenant, the Law is to be written in the heart of the believer.

When Yeshua made the statement that He was the Lord of the Sabbath, He was only confirming that He was YeHoVaH come in the flesh.

Furthermore, the following scripture clearly states that the seventh-day Sabbath is to be kept by **all** nations. Anyone who keeps the covenant will reap the benefits of keeping the covenant.

*Isaiah 56:2-7, "**Blessed is the man that** doeth this, and the son of man that layeth hold on it; that **keepeth the sabbath** from polluting it, and keepeth his hand from doing any evil. Neither let the son of the stranger, that hath joined himself to the LORD, speak, saying, The LORD hath utterly separated me from his people: neither let the eunuch say, Behold, I am a dry tree. For thus saith the LORD unto the eunuchs that keep my sabbaths, and choose the things that please me, and take hold of my covenant; Even unto them will I give in mine house and within my walls a place and a name better* *than of sons and of daughters: I will give them an everlasting name, that shall not be cut off. **Also the sons of the stranger, that join themselves to the LORD, to serve him, and to love the name of the LORD, to be his servants, every one that keepeth the sabbath** from polluting it, and taketh hold of my covenant; Even them will I bring to my holy mountain, and make them joyful in my house of prayer: their burnt offerings and their sacrifices shall be accepted upon mine altar; for mine house shall be called an house of prayer **for all people.***"* KJV*

Arguing that Sunday was the Lord's Day according to Apostle John in *Revelation 1:10*, is in error. It is erroneous to establish a Sunday Sabbath doctrine based upon a single scriptural verse. **This frequently quoted verse does not even specify a day of the week; and is found nowhere else in the entire Bible.**

The Old Testament consequence for breaking the Sabbath is death.

The misleading assumption that the Lord's Day is the first day of the week began as a second century practice of the Roman Catholic Church. The first century writing of the Book of Revelation by Apostle John does not give anyone grounds to conclude that the Apostle John was talking about Sunday.

Now, let us consider another point of view. The Complete Jewish Bible tells us,

Revelation 1:10, *"I came to be, in the Spirit, on the Day of the Lord; and I heard behind me a loud voice, like a trumpet,"* CJB

Every other reference in scripture about "the Day of the Lord" is associated with destruction, war, darkness, doom, the end time, and judgment. There is no verse where

41

it is referred to as the first day of the week, or a day of worship.

Isaiah 13:6, *"Wail, for the day of the LORD is at hand! It will come as destruction from the Almighty." NKJV*

Isaiah 13:9, *"Here comes the Day of Adonai [YeHoVaH], full of cruelty, rage and hot fury, to desolate the earth and destroy the sinners in it." CJB*

Ezekiel 13:5, *"You have not gone up into the gaps to build a wall for the house of Israel to stand in battle on the day of the LORD." NKJV*

Ezekiel 30:3, *"For the day is near, Even the day of the LORD is near; It will be a day of clouds, the time of the Gentiles." NKJV*

Joel 1:15, *"Alas for the day! for the day of the LORD is at hand, and as a destruction from the Almighty shall it come." KJV*

Joel 2:1, *"Blow the trumpet in Zion, And sound an alarm in My holy mountain! Let all the inhabitants of the land tremble; For the day of LORD is coming, For it is at hand:" NKJV*

Joel 2:11, *"Adonai [YeHoVaH] shouts orders to his forces— his army is immense, mighty, and it does what he says. For great is the Day of Adonai [YeHoVaH], fearsome, terrifying! Who can endure it?" CJB*

> *"Hadrian persecuted the Jews in Rome incessantly. In an attempt to separate themselves from the Jews and avoid being persecuted with them, these early Roman Christians began keeping Sunday in addition to the Sabbath."*
> Leo Schreven
> *Now That's Clear: Prophetic Truth Made Simple*

Joel 2:31, *"The sun shall be turned into darkness, and the moon into blood, before the great and terrible day of the LORD come."* KJV

Joel 3:14, *"Multitudes, multitudes in the valley of decision: for the day of the LORD is near in the valley of decision."* KJV

Amos 5:18, *"Woe unto you that desire the day of the LORD! to what end is it for you? the day of the LORD is darkness, and not light."* KJV

Amos 5:20, *"Shall not the day of the LORD be darkness, and not light? even very dark, and no brightness in it?"* KJV

Obadiah 1:15, *"For the day of the LORD is near upon all the heathen: as thou hast done, it shall be done unto thee: thy reward shall return upon thine own head."* KJV

Zephaniah 1:7, *"Keep silent before Adonai [YeHoVaH] ELOHIM, for the Day of ADONAI [YEHOVAH] is near. ADONAI [YEHOVAH] has prepared a sacrifice; he has set apart those he invited."* CJB

Zephaniah 1:14, *"The great day of the LORD is near, it is near, and hasteth greatly, even the voice of the day of the LORD: the mighty man shall cry there bitterly."* KJV

Zechariah 14:1, *"Behold, the day of the LORD cometh, and thy spoil shall be divided in the midst of thee."* KJV

Malachi 4:5, *"Behold, I will send you Elijah the prophet before the coming of the great and dreadful day of the LORD:"* KJV

Acts 2:20, *"The sun will become dark and the moon blood before the great and fearful Day of ADONAI [YEHOVAH] comes."* CJB

1 Corinthians 5:5, *"...hand over such a person to the Adversary for his old nature to be destroyed, so that his spirit may be saved in the Day of the Lord." CJB*

2 Corinthians 1:14, *"...as indeed you have already understood us in part; so that on the Day of our Lord Yeshua you can be as proud of us as we are of you." CJB*

1 Thessalonians 5:2, *"For yourselves know perfectly that the day of the Lord so cometh as a thief in the night." KJV*

2 Thessalonians 2:2, *"...not to be easily shaken in your thinking or anxious because of a spirit or a spoken message or a letter supposedly from us claiming that the Day of the Lord has already come." CJB*

As you can see, the following scriptures are ample evidence that "the Day of the Lord" is not referred to as the first day of the week, or as a day of worship.

Chapter Six

FREQUENTLY ASKED QUESTIONS

Ask, and it shall be given you; seek, and ye shall find;
knock, and it shall be opened unto you:
Matthew 7:7

Is keeping the Sabbath optional?

The Sabbath Law is one of the Ten Commandments.

Exodus 20:8-11, *"Remember the sabbath day, to keep it holy. Six days shalt thou labour, and do all thy work: But the seventh day is the sabbath of the LORD thy God: in it thou shalt not do any work, thou, nor thy son, nor thy daughter, thy manservant, nor thy maidservant, nor thy cattle, nor thy stranger that is within thy gates: For in six days the LORD made heaven and earth, the sea, and all that in them is, and rested the seventh day: wherefore the LORD blessed the sabbath day, and hallowed it." KJV*

Can I choose any day to be my Sabbath?

NO! God calls the Sabbath **His** holy day; not ours.

Isaiah 58:13, *"If thou turn away thy foot from the sabbath, from doing thy pleasure on my holy day; and call the sabbath a delight, the holy of the LORD, honourable; and shalt honour him, not doing thine own ways, nor finding thine own pleasure, nor speaking thine own words." KJV*

God only gives us grace (divine ability) to do what He commands us to do.

Do you know any believers who really observe the Sabbath according to the guidelines of Law/Torah?

Is there a penalty for not keeping the Sabbath?

The Old Testament consequence for breaking the Sabbath was death.

Exodus 31:15, *"Six days may work be done; but in the seventh is the sabbath of rest, holy to the LORD: whosoever doeth any work in the sabbath day, he shall surely be put to death." KJV*

Exodus 35:2, *"Six days shall work be done, but on the seventh day there shall be to you a holy day, a sabbath of rest to the LORD: whosoever doeth work therein shall be put to death." KJV*

We also see the death penalty instituted when someone was found gathering sticks on the Sabbath.

Numbers 15:36, *"And all the congregation brought him without the camp, and stoned him with stones, and he died; as the LORD commanded Moses." KJV*

Is one day just as good as another to rest?

Genesis 2:2-3, *"And on the seventh day God ended his work which he had made; and he rested on the seventh day from all his work which he had made. And God blessed the seventh day, and sanctified it: because that in it he had rested from all his work which God created and made." KJV*

Exodus 20:9-11, *"Six days shalt thou labour, and do all thy work: But the seventh day is the sabbath of the LORD thy God: in it thou shalt not do any work, thou, nor thy son, nor thy daughter, thy manservant, nor thy maidservant, nor thy cattle, nor thy stranger that is within thy gates: For in six days the LORD made heaven and earth, the sea, and all that in them is, and rested the seventh day: wherefore the LORD blessed the sabbath day, and hallowed it." KJV*

Today worldwide, Saturday is still considered the seventh; and Sunday the first day of the week. The word "hallow" or "holy" means "to be set apart." Because God rested on the seventh day, this made the seventh day different from all the other days; and a day where He did not work

The Sabbath is for everyone, and not just for the Jews.

at all. Also in Leviticus, the Bible states:

> **Leviticus 23:3**, *"Six days shall work be done: but the seventh day is the sabbath of rest, an holy convocation; ye shall do no work therein: it is the sabbath of the* LORD *in all your dwellings." KJV*

Isn't every day blessed?

Only the seventh day was blessed by the Creator during the seven days of creation. YeHoVaH did not bless the first six days of creation. This fact has never changed. Even Paul states:

> **Romans14:5-6**, *"One person considers some days more holy than others, while someone else regards them as being all alike. What is important is for each to be fully convinced in his own mind. He who observes a day as special does so to honor the Lord. Also he who eats anything, eats to honor the Lord, since he gives thanks to God; likewise the abstainer abstains to honor the Lord, and he too gives thanks to God." CJB*

The Sabbath was sanctified, set apart, and declared holy. **Only** the seventh day was blessed and declared holy by the creator during the seven days of creation. Man may declare a day holy; but that does not mean that YeHoVaH agrees or confirms man's declaration.

> ***Genesis 2:2-3**, "And on the seventh day God ended his work which he had made; and he rested on the seventh day from all his work which he had made. And God blessed the seventh day, and sanctified it: because that in it he had rested from all his work which God created and made." KJV*

Is the keeping of the Law/Torah for our benefit?

Yes, the keeping of the Law/Torah is for our benefit that it may **be well** with us.

> ***Deuteronomy 6:24**, "And the LORD commanded us to do all these statutes, to fear the LORD our God, for our good always, that he might preserve us alive, as it is at this day." KJV*

> ***Deuteronomy 5:33,** "Ye shall walk in all the ways which the LORD your God hath commanded you, that ye may live, and that it may be well with you, and that ye may prolong your days in the land which ye shall possess." KJV*

In the last chapter of the last book of the New Testament, God explicitly states that there is a blessing for those who keep the Commandments.

> ***Revelation 22:14**, "Blessed are they that do his commandments that they may have right to the tree of life, and may enter in through the gates into the city." KJV*

Is the Sabbath a day for rest "only"?

The Sabbath was more than just a day of rest. It was also a sacred assembly for the people of YeHoVaH.

"...thus have ye made the commandment of God of none effect by your tradition."
Matthew 15:6b

48

Hebrews 10:24-25, *"And let us consider one another in order to stir up love and good works, not forsaking the assembling of ourselves together, as is the manner of some, but exhorting one another, and so much the more as you see the Day approaching." CJB*

Did Sabbath observance cease with the New Testament?

In any legal system, a statute continues to be in effect until it is repealed. Therefore the Sabbath is to be perpetually observed.

Exodus 31:16, *"Wherefore the children of Israel shall keep the sabbath, to observe the sabbath throughout their generations, for a perpetual covenant." KJV*

The observance of the Sabbath as one of the Commandments is even mentioned during the seven years of tribulation; which is yet to come.

Revelation 14:12, *"Here is the patience of the saints: here are they that keep the commandments of God, and the faith of Jesus [Yeshua]." KJV*

Didn't Yeshua come to destroy the keeping of the Law/Torah?

NO! Yeshua said:

Matthew 5:17-19, *"Think not that I am come to destroy the law [Torah], or the prophets: I am not come to destroy, but to fulfill. For verily I say unto you, till heaven and earth pass, one jot or one tittle shall in no wise pass from the law [Torah], till all be fulfilled. Whosoever therefore shall break one of these least commandments, and shall teach men so, he shall be called the least in the kingdom of heaven: but whosoever shall do and teach them, the same shall be called great in the kingdom of heaven." KJV*

Three points are to be observed from the above scripture:

- *Yeshua came to fulfill the Law/Torah.*

- *He said that the Law/Torah would not pass away until "all be fulfilled." There are still End-Time prophecies yet to be fulfilled.*

- *He that keeps the Law/Torah and teaches others to do so will be called great in the kingdom of heaven.*

What does it mean that Yeshua came to fulfill the Law/Torah? The very wording of the passage suggests that the Law/Torah was not done away with. Paul's writing gives us the answer.

> ***Romans 8:1-8***, *"Therefore, there is no longer any condemnation awaiting those who are in union with the Messiah Yeshua. Why? Because the Torah [Law] of the Spirit, which produces this life in union with Messiah Yeshua, has set me free from the "Torah" [Law] of sin and death. For what the Torah [Law] could not do by itself, because it lacked the power to make the old nature cooperate, God did by sending his own Son as a human being with a nature like our own sinful one [but without sin]. God did this in order to deal with sin, and in so doing he executed the punishment against sin in human nature, so that the just requirement of the Torah [Law] might be fulfilled in us who do not run our lives according to what our old nature wants but according to what the Spirit wants. For those who identify with their old nature set their minds on the things of the old nature, but those who identify with the Spirit set their minds on the things of the Spirit. Having one's mind controlled by the old nature is death, but having one's mind controlled by the Spirit is life and shalom. For the mind controlled by the old nature is hostile to God, because it does not submit itself to God's Torah [Law] — indeed, it cannot. Thus, those who identify with their old nature cannot please God." CJB*

Did Yeshua and the Apostles keep the Sabbath?

YES! It was the "custom" of Yeshua to observe the Sabbath.

> **Luke 4:16**, *"And he came to Nazareth, where he had been brought up: and, as his custom was, he went into the synagogue on the sabbath day, and stood up for to read." KJV*

Wasn't the Sabbath changed from Saturday to Sunday because Yeshua arose from the grave on the first day of the week?

Let's consider what possible bearing the day of Yeshua's resurrection could have on the day the Sabbath is to be celebrated. Other than church tradition, there is no reason for changing the Sabbath day – certainly none to be found in the Bible. (See the next chapter for more information on this.)

Based upon crucifixion facts, another important question arises. "Is it even true that Yeshua was resurrected on Sunday?" Notice what Yeshua told the Pharisees, who were looking for a sign of the Messiah:

> **Matthew 12:39-40**, *"But he answered and said unto them, An evil and adulterous generation seeketh after a sign; and there shall no sign be given to it, but the sign of the prophet Jonas: For as Jonas was three days and three nights in the whale's belly; so shall the Son of man be three days and three nights in the heart of the earth." KJV*

The only sign that Yeshua gave to prove that He was the Messiah, was that the grave would only hold Him for a limited amount of time – exactly "three days and three nights," or seventy-two hours.

However, those who keep the Easter Sunday tradition maintain that Yeshua was buried just before sunset on "Good Friday" afternoon, and resurrected early Sunday morning. This logic accounts for only two nights and one day, or thirty-six hours!

Some argue the definition of the word "day." They cite rabbinical or Jewish tradition which dictates that any part of a day is considered the whole day. Thus a part of Friday, all day Saturday, and then a part of Sunday constitutes three days. Yeshua did not say that He would be in the heart of the earth a part of three days and a part of two nights, but three days and three nights.

In *John 11:9-10*, Yeshua clearly stated that there were twelve hours in a day, not including the night. Three days and three nights are seventy-two hours. But was it exactly seventy-two hours?

Yeshua said that He would arise "AFTER three days" (*Mark 8:31*). This means it would occur in no less than seventy-two hours. He also said in *John 2:19-21*, that He would rise "in three days," which is no more than seventy-two hours. This is absolutely clear to mean exactly seventy-two hours! *And YeHoVaH is always right on schedule.*

Also consider that when the women came to His tomb

We should not follow hundreds of years of church tradition by keeping Sunday as the Sabbath.

Sunday morning, "it was still dark" (*John 20:1*) and He had already risen. How could this be possible?

The Sunday-resurrection proponents contend that He had risen just moments before. If they were correct, then "three days and three nights" earlier would mean just before sunrise on Thursday morning.

No one believes that Yeshua was buried on Thursday morning; or any morning for that matter, and with good reason. When Joseph of Arimathaea laid Yeshua's body in the tomb, "the Sabbath drew near" (*Luke 23:50-54*). Biblical days including Sabbaths, begin at sunset and end the following sunset (*Genesis 1:5-31; Leviticus 23:32*). They include a nighttime period followed by a daytime period.

Yeshua then was buried in late afternoon, before a particular Sabbath began at sunset. Three days and three nights later would be the same time of day, or late afternoon! Now we have another problem. If we assume that Yeshua was buried on Friday afternoon, as the Good Friday tradition asserts, then His resurrection seventy-two hours later would have been on Monday afternoon. Yet again no one believes this either, and with good reason. Remember that Yeshua had already risen before the women came to His tomb prior to daybreak Sunday morning! What then, is the answer?

Why have so many thought that Yeshua was put in the grave on Friday afternoon? *Mark 15:42* states that "it was the Preparation Day, that is, the day before the Sabbath." Since the weekly Sabbath was always observed on the seventh day of the week, now called Saturday, the "Preparation Day" was normally on

The reason the Son of God appeared was to destroy the devil's work.

Friday. However, we have already seen the problem with this.

The answer to the apparent dilemma is that the weekly Sabbath is not the only Sabbath mentioned in the Bible. *Leviticus 23* lists seven annual Holy Days that occur during YeHoVaH's Festivals. Each of these days was considered as a Sabbath, meaning a "rest" from normal labor. All annual Sabbaths or "High Days," except for Pentecost fell on particular calendar dates rather than set days of the week.

Now the mystery can be solved by reading the following verse.

> **John 19:31**, *"Therefore, because it was the Preparation Day, that the bodies should not remain on the cross on the Sabbath (for that Sabbath was a high day), the Jews asked Pilate that their legs might be broken, and that they might be taken away." NKJV*

Yeshua died on the cross on Passover – the 14th of *Abib* or *Nisan* according to the Hebrew Calendar:

> **Leviticus 23:5-7**, *"In the fourteenth day of the first month at even is the LORD's passover. And on the fifteenth day of the same month is the feast of unleavened bread unto the LORD: seven days ye must eat unleavened bread. In the first day ye shall have an holy convocation: ye shall do no servile work therein." KJV*

These scriptures also report that the next day, (beginning the evening after His crucifixion) was not a weekly Sabbath, but an annual Sabbath – the first day of the Feast of Unleavened Bread.

Let us put together the facts. From the Bible we clearly understand that Yeshua died and was buried on Passover afternoon, and that the following day was an annual Sabbath. It is also clear that he was resurrected at the same time of day – late afternoon. But which afternoon is the question.

Since the women found Him already gone Sunday morning, it would be sensible to conclude that He had been resurrected the previous afternoon on Saturday! This would mean that He was buried three days and three nights earlier, on Wednesday afternoon. It would also mean that Passover, *Nisan 14*, fell on a Wednesday that year. And indeed, that is what happened in A.D. 28 (Michael Rood, *The Chronological Gospels*, 2013, p. 259); a year that fits the time frame the Bible demands.

Scripture also provides further proof that there were **TWO** Sabbaths that week; an annual, and a weekly one. In *Mark 15:47*, Mary Magdalene and her companion watched Joseph of Arimathaea lay Yeshua in the tomb near the end of the Passover.

The next verse, *Mark 16:1* tells us that **after the** "Sabbath," Mary Magdalene and her companions bought spices with which to anoint Yeshua's dead body. However, *Luke 23:56* shows that they prepared the spices **before the Sabbath**. Naturally, they could not have prepared spices before they even bought them! The only explanation that makes sense is that they bought the spices on Friday and prepared them the same day, after the annual Sabbath (first day of the Feast of Unleavened Bread) which was on Thursday and before the weekly

The disciples did not change the Sabbath day (Saturday) to the first day (Sunday).

55

Sabbath on Saturday! Then they rested on the weekly Sabbath, the day on which Yeshua was resurrected. The next morning was Sunday, when they came to the tomb before sunrise and found him already gone.

Some will point out *Mark 16:9*, which says, *"Now when He rose early on the first day of the week..." (NKJV)* Yet how can this be evidence? To understand better, we should read the verse in the original King James Version and continue further in the sentence: *"Now when Yeshua was risen...* [the perfect tense is correct here; He was already risen] *...early the first day of the week, he appeared first to Mary Magdalene."*

He was not "rising" on Sunday morning. As we have seen, He rose on Saturday afternoon. So early Sunday morning, He was already "risen." Realize also that in the original Greek, there were no punctuation marks. Had the King James translators simply put a comma after the word "risen" and not after "week," this would have made complete sense. The Centenary Translation renders it this way: *"Now after his resurrection, early on the first day of the week He appeared first to Mary Magdalene."*

In conclusion, a Sunday morning resurrection could not be the reason for changing the weekly day of worship from Saturday to Sunday.

But even if Yeshua were resurrected on Sunday, why would His disciples, who had kept the seventh-day Sabbath with Him, have abandoned His example of keeping the Ten Commandments and switched to Sunday-keeping? And why would they have picked Sunday, a day already associated with pagan sun worship? The Bible is very clear that Yeshua was not resurrected on Sunday morning. Thus, this attempt to change YeHoVaH's Law/Torah has no merit!

No man has authority to change the Commandments of YeHoVaH. YeHoVaH is the only Lawgiver.

> ***James 4:12a***, *"There is but one Giver of Torah [Law]; he is also the Judge, with the power to deliver and to destroy." CJB*

Is the Christian church wrong to keep Sunday as the Sabbath?

We should not follow hundreds of years of church tradition by keeping

Anyone who says, "I know him," but isn't obeying his commands is a liar — the truth is not in him.
1 John 2:4, CJB

Sunday as the Sabbath. We are not to follow the traditions of men, especially when they contradict the Word of God.

> ***Matthew 15:6b***, *"Thus have ye made the commandment of God of none effect by your tradition." KJV*

> ***Mark 7:13***, *"Making the word of God of none effect through your tradition, which ye have delivered: and many such like things do ye." KJV*

John defines sin as lawlessness. The question becomes "What is lawlessness?" It is to be without Law/Torah. "Which law?" God's Law/Torah.

According to Paul in his letter to Rome:

> ***Romans 4:15***, *"For what law [Torah] brings is punishment. But where there is no law [Torah], there is also no violation." CJB*

Romans 5:13, *"Sin was indeed present in the world before Torah [Law] was given, but sin is not counted as such when there is no Torah [Law]." CJB*

Will the Sabbath be observed during the future reign of Yeshua?

Yes, it will.

Isaiah 66:22-23, *"For as the new heavens and the new earth, which I will make, shall remain before me, saith the LORD, so shall your seed and your name remain. And it shall come to pass, that from one new moon to another, and from one sabbath to another, shall all flesh come to worship before me, saith the LORD." KJV*

As a part of the New Covenant, the Law/Torah has been written in the heart of believers.

Ezekiel 36:27, *"And I will put my spirit within you, and cause you to walk in my statutes, and ye shall keep my judgments, and do them." KJV*

Hebrews 8:10, *"For this is the covenant that I will make with the house of Israel after those days, saith the Lord; I will put my Laws [Torah] into their mind, and write them in their hearts: and I will be to them a God, and they shall be to me a people." KJV*

Did the disciples change the Sabbath Day to Sunday?

The disciples did not change the Sabbath (Saturday) to the first day of the week (Sunday). Acts carries a record of the disciples eating together on the first day of the week while Paul preached to them.

Acts 20:7, *"And upon the first day of the week, when the disciples came together to break bread, Paul preached unto* *them, ready to depart on the morrow; and continued his speech until midnight." KJV*

The first day of the week mentioned here is actually Saturday after sundown. This was the traditional Jewish end-of-Sabbath meal. Even if it were Sunday morning, nothing is mentioned about changing the Sabbath or making Sunday the Sabbath.

In Corinthians, while Paul was raising funds for the Messianic Community in Jerusalem, he instructed the individuals to put aside a mission offering on the first day of the week. This would make it easy for him to collect when he came.

The Sabbath is to be perpetually observed.

I Corinthians 16:2, "Upon the first day of the week let every one of you lay by him in store, as God hath prospered him, that there be no gatherings when I come." KJV

This passage does not indicate whether they met together, but rather that an offering was laid aside on an individual basis. It may have been that some believers went from house to house gathering the offering. It may be that they did not go about to collect the offering on the Sabbath as the people did not collect the manna on the Sabbath. This was purely an organizational administrative instruction.

Did Paul observe the Sabbath?

Acts 17:2, "And Paul, as his manner was, went in unto them, and three sabbath days reasoned with them out of the scriptures." KJV

Acts 18:4, "And he reasoned in the synagogue every sabbath, and persuaded the Jews and the Greeks." KJV

Did Paul keep the Sabbath on Sunday?

Many Christian theologians teach that Paul in Colossians forbade the observance of the Sabbath. However Paul said:

> **Colossians 2:16-17**, *"So let no one judge you in food or in drink, or regarding a festival or a new moon or sabbaths, which are a shadow of things to come, but the substance is of Christ [Messiah]."* NKJV

This passage used to pose a problem to me concerning the observance of the Sabbath. It seemed to contradict other scriptures. There are basically two views to take into consideration when explaining this passage.

First from a western church perspective (which is the most popular view), Paul is certainly condemning the Law/Torah concerning the observing of holy days, new moons and Sabbath days.

The western church view further supports its position by invoking what Paul says in verse 14:

> **Colossians 2:14**, *"Blotting out the handwriting of ordinances that was against us, which was contrary to us, and took it out of the way, nailing it to his cross."* KJV

However the whole statement should be viewed against the backdrop of Paul's opening warning:

> **Colossians 2:8**, *"Beware lest any man spoil you through philosophy and vain deceit, after the tradition of men, after the rudiments of the world, and not after Christ [Messiah]."* KJV

Although the western church stance is the most popular view, it is certainly wrong.

I call the second view the scriptural or biblical view. This view takes in account who wrote the letter, to whom it was written, and why.

It appears from *Colossians 2:1* that Paul himself had never preached in Colosse. It was Epaphras, a native of Colosse (*Colossians 4:12*), a fellow servant and a faithful minister of Messiah who taught in Colosse (*Colossians 1:7*).

More than likely, Epaphras informed Paul of the potential influences in and around the Colossian and Laodicean communities. This is surmised because Paul requested that his letter to each Messianic Community be read in both communities (*Colossians 4:16*).

Next we must note that nowhere is the letter to the Colossian Messianic Community addressing the Law/Torah of YeHoVaH. Paul is addressing some form of erroneous mystic teachings that were being taught. In the letter to the Colossians Paul states:

Colossians 2:8, *"Beware lest any man spoil you through philosophy and vain deceit, after the tradition of men, after the rudiments of the world, and not after the Messiah."* KJV

Colossians 2:18, *"Let no man beguile you of your reward in a voluntary humility and worshipping of angels, intruding into those things which he hath not seen, vainly puffed up by his fleshly mind."* KJV

If Paul is not addressing the Law/Torah, then what is he saying when he writes the verse below?

Colossians 2:14, *"Blotting out the handwriting of ordinances that was against us, which was contrary to us, and took it out of the way, nailing it to his cross."* KJV

Paul is talking about being forgiven of the trespasses mentioned in verse 13!

Colossians 2:13, *"And you, being dead in your sins and the uncircumcision of your flesh, hath he quickened together with him, having forgiven you all trespasses."* *KJV*

When a criminal was executed on a stake, it was customary to nail a list of his crimes on the stake. An example is the sign that was placed above Yeshua's head (*John 19:19-22*). According to *Matthew 1:21b*, the Messiah came to "save His people from their sins." Through His death, by shedding His blood to atone for our sins, He forgave us and **nailed our sins to the cross**.

The Law/Torah required a bull to be sacrificed for the sins of Israel (*Exodus 29:10-14*). It was "a sin offering." Messiah Yeshua became that sin offering; thereby fulfilling the requirement of that portion of the Law/Torah (*Hebrews 10:5-10*).

It was not the Law/Torah that was nailed to the cross, but the mandatory traditions of men that were nailed to the cross. Therefore in going to the cross, he disarmed principalities and powers and made a public spectacle of them; triumphing over them as mentioned in:

Colossians 2:14, *"Blotting out the handwriting of ordinances that was against us, which was contrary to us, and took it out of the way, nailing it to his cross;"KJV*

Yeshua had not come to "abolish the Law/Torah" (*Matthew 5:17*), or to take it away. He came to take away our *sins*, which is what John said.

1 John 3:4-5, *"Everyone who keeps sinning is violating Torah [Law] — indeed, sin is violation of Torah [Law]. You know that he [Yeshua] appeared in order to take away sins, and that there is no sin in him." CJB*

He came to free us from the control of the devil because:

1 John 3:8, *"He that committeth sin is of the devil; for the devil sinneth from the beginning. For this purpose the Son of God was manifested, that he might destroy the works of the devil." KJV*

In order to understand what Paul really meant when he wrote "let no man judge you in food or in drink, or "regarding a festival or a new moon or Sabbaths," we need to remember Ground Rules 1 and 2.

Rule 1: These believers only had the Old Testament as scripture. **Rule 2:** They were learning Law/Torah, which contained commandments about Sabbath, holy days, and what was and was not considered as food. (By the way, only the Old Testament defines what food is. See *Genesis 1:29* and *Leviticus 11: 1- 47*.)

These Gentile believers were turning to the **truth** and away from their pagan practices. They were observing the mandated feasts and Sabbaths, and probably causing people who had known them all their lives to condemn the new religion and its practices because it was so different from the religions of the country.

The Messiah came to save His people from their sins.

These new believers were faced with some of the same challenges we face daily from our family members and friends. Paul therefore wrote to them to encourage them as they were embracing the teachings of Law/Torah. **He cautioned them not to let the pagans judge them and to persuade them against the Law/Torah**.

Just as the Hebrew people were honoring the Commandments concerning food and drinks, the holy days, and festivals in obedience to YeHoVaH's Law/Torah; now these Gentile believers were being brought near through the blood of Messiah.

Ephesians 2:11-13, *"Wherefore remember, that ye being in time past Gentiles in the flesh, who are called Uncircumcision by that which is called the Circumcision in the flesh made by hands; That at that time ye were without Christ [Messiah], being aliens from the commonwealth of Israel, and strangers from the covenants of promise, having no hope, and without God in the world: But now in Christ Jesus[Messiah Yeshua] ye who sometimes were far off are made nigh by the blood of Christ [Messiah]." KJV*

"Most Christians assume that Sunday is the biblically approved day of worship. The Roman Catholic Church protests that it transferred Christian worship from the biblical Sabbath (Saturday) to Sunday, and that to try to argue that the change was made in the Bible is both dishonest and a denial of Catholic authority."
<http://www.immaculateheart.com>

We should not continue to follow hundreds of years of church tradition in keeping the Sabbath on Sunday. **Traditions of men should not be followed when they contradict the Word of YeHoVaH.**

Matthew 15:6b, "Thus have ye made the commandment of God of none effect by your tradition." KJV

Yeshua further stated:

Mark 7:13, "Making the word of God of none effect through your tradition, which ye have delivered: and many such like things do ye." KJV

Matthew 15:9, "But in vain they do worship me, teaching for doctrines the commandments of men." KJV

Following traditions of men renders our worship ineffective. True worshippers worship in spirit and in truth. There is no truth in the traditions of men when they add to, or subtract from the commands of YeHoVaH.

Deuteronomy 4:2, "Ye shall not add unto the word which I command you, neither shall ye diminish ought from it, that ye may keep the commandments of the LORD your God which I command you." KJV

History shows that Sunday worship replacing the seventh-day Sabbath is a tradition of men, and specifically the early Roman church. The fall of Jerusalem in 68 A.D. was followed by a violent attack on believers worldwide. Until then, Jerusalem had been the headquarters of the Messianic community. All the hard questions concerning non-Israelite believers were sent to the apostles in Jerusalem for answers.

After the fall of Jerusalem, Rome (being the capital of the world), became the next capital for the Messianic community by default. With the mounting anti-Semitic influence in Rome, this was not a good forecast for the future of the Messianic community. Emperor Claudius exiled all Jews, including Messianic Jews, out of Rome. Among those were Aquila and Priscilla. The Roman Messianic community was left to the leadership of newly converted Messianic Gentiles.

Later when some Jewish believers were returning to Rome, they were confronted with a Gentile-led Messianic community. This was not a problem until Rome waged war with the Jews. At that time, the fledgling Gentile-led Messianic community was struggling with identity issues and being plagued by heresies and persecution. Every emperor from Nero (who martyred Paul and Peter), to Domitian (who exiled Apostle John to the Isle of Patmos), had persecuted the apostles and Messianic community leaders alike.

The result was the rise of anti-Semitic sentiment, even among newly converted pagans in the Messianic communities. There was a notion that God had replaced Israel as his chosen people with Gentile believers; a sentiment that still prevails in the present day church. Being

Messianic and studying the Law/Torah became an antithesis with being Christian; thus enlarging the chasm between the Israelite and Gentile believers.

In the second century, Emperor Hadrian decided to wage another war with the Jews. He aimed to capture Jerusalem and to build a pagan temple on the site of the previously destroyed temple. The Jews waged such a resistance that he returned home humiliated. In retaliation, the emperor made a law declaring the observance of the Sabbath as illegal.

The Gentile believers of those days are the men that today we call the Church Fathers. Among them was Ignatius, who wrote in an epistle to Asian believers condemning the observance of the Sabbath according to the Law/Torah (The Epistle of Ignatius to the Magnesians, Chapter 8).

"Be not deceived with strange doctrines, nor with old fables, which are unprofitable. For if we still live according to the Jewish law, we acknowledge that we have not received grace."

Ignatius further stated:

"Let us therefore no longer keep the Sabbath after the Jewish manner, and rejoice in days of idleness; for 'he that does not work, let him not eat.' For say the (holy) oracles, 'In the sweat of thy face shalt thou eat thy bread.' But let every one of you keep the Sabbath after a spiritual

And it shall come to pass, that from one new moon to another, and from one sabbath to another, all flesh shall come to worship before me, saith the LORD.
Isaiah 66:23, KJV

manner, rejoicing in meditation on the law, not in relaxation of the body, admiring the workmanship of God, and not eating things prepared the day before, nor using lukewarm drinks, and walking within a prescribed space, nor finding delight in dancing and plaudits which have no sense in them. And after the observance of the Sabbath, let every friend of Christ [Messiah] keep the Lord's Day as a festival, the resurrection-day, the queen and chief of all the days (of the week)."

It was after this era that we find the rise of the heretic, Marcion. He proposed a theology which had an Old Testament God and a New Testament God. According to this new theology, Jesus had unseated the Old Testament God, the God of the Jews. Thus Marcion advocated and the church accepted the abolition of the relics of the Jewish culture associated with the Christian faith.

The celebration of the Sabbath on Saturday was replaced by Sunday worship, supposedly commemorating the resurrection of the Messiah each week. (Oddly, the Messiah rose only one day of the year; yet the observance was weekly.)

The day chosen happened to coincide with the day of sun worship, or Sunday. To this was added the celebration of the birth of the sun god on December 25th, which was adopted as the birth of the Messiah. Is it not interesting that the sun god became the symbol for the Messiah? Christians still hold onto these man-made holy days instead of the Sabbath and the Feasts of YeHoVaH!

These man-made traditions became a key subject at the Council of Trent, held in northeast Italy (1545 to 1563). The papal representative, the Archbishop of Reggio, silenced the "scripture only" arguments of Martin Luther and the Protestant "reformers," when he correctly stated:

"The Protestants claim to stand upon the written word only; they profess to hold the Scriptures alone as the standard of faith. They justify their revolt by the plea that the Catholic Church has apostatized from the written word and follows tradition. Now the Protestants' claim that they stand upon the written word alone is not true. Their profession of holding the Scriptures alone as the standard of faith is false. Proof...The written word explicitly enjoins the observance of the seventh day as the Sabbath. They do not observe the seventh day, but reject it. If they truly hold the Scriptures alone as the standard, they would be observing the seventh day as it is enjoined in the Scripture throughout. Yet they not only reject the observance of the Sabbath as enjoined in the written word, but they have adopted, and do practice, the observance of Sunday, for which they have only the tradition of the (Catholic) Church. Consequently, the claim of Scripture alone as the standard fails and the doctrine of 'Scripture and tradition as essential' is fully established, the Protestants themselves being Judges."

"And what wisdom is this which is given unto him, that even such mighty works are wrought by his hands?"
Mark 6:2b

69

Chapter Eight

OBSERVING THE SABBATH

"And where are we told in the Scriptures that we are to keep the first day at all? We are commanded to keep the seventh; but we are nowhere commanded to keep the first day."
Isaac Williams
Plain Sermons on the Catechism, pp. 334, 336.

Keeping the Sabbath is not only for Jews.

YeHoVaH established Sabbath at the end of creation, long before the Jewish people came into existence. Yeshua said the Sabbath was made for <u>man</u>, not just for <u>Jews</u>. The word "Jew" is not even mentioned in the Bible until II Kings.

Mark 2:27, "And he said unto them, The sabbath was made for man, and not man for the sabbath." KJV

Paul brought the whole city together, both Jews and Gentiles, on the Sabbath.

Acts 13:14, 42, and 44, "But when they departed from Perga, they came to Antioch in Pisidia, and went into the synagogue on the sabbath day, and sat down...And when the Jews were gone out of the synagogue, the Gentiles besought that these words might be preached to them the next Sabbath...And the next sabbath day came almost the whole city together to hear the word of God." KJV

Furthermore the Sabbath Law is one of the Ten Commandments which is for everyone; not just Jews.

Please note that according to the New International

Version (NIV) Study Bible (Kenneth Barker, Zondervan Publishing House):

- *The term "Jew" (Hebrew: Yehudi, Greek: Ioudaios, Latin: Judaeus) does not occur before the period of Jeremiah in Old Testament literature. Originally, it denoted one belonging to the tribe of Judah or to the two tribes of the southern kingdom (2 Kings 16:6; 25:25). Later it was applied to anyone of the Hebrew race who returned from the Babylonian captivity. As most of the exiles came from Judah, and because they were the main historical representatives of ancient Israel, the term "Jew" finally came to mean the entire Hebrew race throughout the world (Esther 2:5; Matt 2:2).*

- *As early as the days of Hezekiah, the language of Judah was called Jewish. (In the NIV, it is called Hebrew.) In the Old Testament, the adjective applies only to the Jews' language or speech (2 Kings 18:26,28; Nehemiah 13:24; Isaiah 36:11,13).*

- *In the Gospels, Jews (always plural, except for John 4:9; 18:35) is the usual term for Israelites. Also in the New Testament, Jews (Israelites) and Gentiles are sometimes contrasted (Mark 7:3; John 2:6; Acts 10:28).*

- *Paul warns against Jewish myths (Titus 1:14) and speaks of the Jews' religion (Galatians 1:13-14).*

Keeping the Sabbath is also for Gentiles.

In *Isaiah 56* we find a remarkable prophecy set right in the midst of End-Time Prophecies; many of which refer to the years just ahead. In this setting, YeHoVaH gives this pointed instruction to men and women of ALL nations:

> **Isaiah 56:2**, *"Blessed is the man who does this, and the son of man who lays hold on it; who keeps from defiling the sabbath, and keeps his hand from doing any evil." KJV*

A few verses later, YeHoVaH instructs the Gentiles or foreigners to keep His Sabbath, and describes the **blessings** that would come from doing so:

Isaiah 56:6-7, *"Also the sons of the foreigner Who join themselves to the LORD, to serve Him, And to love the name of the LORD, to be His servants—Everyone who keeps from defiling the Sabbath, And holds fast My covenant—Even them I will bring to My holy mountain, And make them joyful in My house of prayer. Their burnt offerings and their sacrifices Will be accepted on My altar; For My house shall be called a house of prayer for all nations."* NKJV

In another inspired End-Time Prophecy, YeHoVaH's Word shows that His true servants will be keeping the Sabbath day holy even during the 1,000-year reign of Yeshua on earth:

Isaiah 66:22-23, *"'For as the new heavens and the new earth Which I will make shall remain before Me,' says the LORD, 'So shall your descendants and your name remain. And it shall come to pass That from one New Moon to another, And from one Sabbath to another, All flesh shall come to worship before Me,' says the LORD."* NKJV

Obedience to the Fourth Commandment is not "old-fashioned." Instead it is "the wave of the future!" When the Kingdom of YeHoVaH is set up on this earth, **all humanity** will learn to obey His Commandments and keep holy the days **YeHoVaH made holy**!

All true followers of the Messiah keep the seventh-day Sabbath Commandment.

Throughout the Bible, YeHoVaH indicates that His true followers keep His commandments. For example in *Revelation 12*, YeHoVaH describes the true Messianic

73

community as the little flock that had to escape the bonds of the Roman Empire during the Dark Ages (v. 6). Then He foretells how this will happen again in our day (v. 14). Finally YeHoVaH describes Satan's rage against the Messianic Community:

> **Revelation12:17**, *"The dragon was infuriated over the woman and went off to fight the rest of her children, those who obey God's commands and bear witness to Yeshua."* CJB

God describes the character of His saints by saying:

> **Revelation 14:12**, *"This is when perseverance is needed on the part of God's people, those who observe his commands and exercise Yeshua's faithfulness."* CJB

Notice that the saints do not merely observe some "new" Commandments of Yeshua. They observe **YeHoVaH's Commandments** through the **faith OF Yeshua Ha Mashiach** (Yeshua, The Messiah), not merely their **faith IN Yeshua.**

> **Galatians 2:20**, *"I am crucified with Christ [Messiah]: nevertheless I live; yet not I, but Christ [Messiah] liveth in me: and the life which I now live in the flesh I live by the faith of the Son of God, who loved me, and gave himself for me."* KJV

Through the Holy Spirit, we have Yeshua living **His** life in us and empowering us to overcome ourselves, the world, and Satan. We are therefore able to OBEY YeHoVaH's spiritual Law/Torah!

The following verse describes those who will live with YeHoVaH the Father and Yeshua throughout eternity in the New Jerusalem:

Revelation 22:14, *"Blessed are those who **DO HIS COMMANDMENTS,** that they may have the right to the tree of life, and may enter through the gates into the city." KJV*

<u>Keeping the Fourth Commandment seventh-day Sabbath IS a SALVATION issue.</u>

Yeshua said:

John 14:15, "If ye love me, keep my commandments." KJV

John emphatically states:

1 John 2:3-4, "Now by this we know that we know Him, if we keep His commandments. He who says, 'I know Him,' and does not keep His commandments, is a liar, and the truth is not in him." NKJV

Again, as John wrote, God's very LOVE is expressed in the Ten Commandments.

1 John 5:3, "For this is the love of God, that we keep his commandments. And his commandments are not burdensome." KJV

Anyone who fails to literally keep the Law/Torah as a way of life is **DISOBEYING** his Creator and in fact, does not really "know" God!

"The seventh day, the commandment says, is the Sabbath of the Lord thy God. No kind of arithmetic, no kind of almanac, can make seven equal one, nor the seventh mean the first, nor Saturday mean Sunday...The fact is that we are all Sabbath breakers, everyone of us."
Rev George Hodges, Church of England

Chapter Nine

SCRIPTURAL GUIDELINES FOR THE SABBATH

"But if ye will not hearken unto me to hallow the sabbath day, and not to bear a burden, even entering in at the gates of Jerusalem on the sabbath day; then will I kindle a fire in the gates thereof, and it shall devour the palaces of Jerusalem, and it shall not be quenched." Jeremiah 17:27

We are to remember the Sabbath.

The Sabbath is first mentioned in Genesis when God rested from his work of creation. The Fourth Commandment, Sabbath, is the only one of the Ten that YeHoVaH says that we are specifically to remember.

Exodus 20:8, "Remember the sabbath day, to keep it holy." KJV

"Remember" implies that the practice of observing the Sabbath preceded the giving of the Law/Torah in *Exodus 20*. In *Exodus 16*, Moses gave all of the people; Israelites and foreigners, instructions concerning what they were to do on the Sabbath.

Exodus 16:22-23, "And it came to pass, that on the sixth day they gathered twice as much bread, two omers for one man: and all the rulers of the congregation came and told Moses. And he said unto them, This is that which the LORD hath said, To morrow is the rest of the holy sabbath unto the LORD: bake that which ye will bake to day, and seethe that ye will seethe; and that which remaineth over lay up for you to be kept until the morning." KJV

Maybe YeHoVaH said to <u>remember the Sabbath</u> because He knew how easy it would be for us to forget it.

We are to do no work on the Sabbath or have others work for us.

Exodus 20:10, *"But the seventh day is the sabbath of the LORD thy God: in it thou shalt not do any work, thou, nor thy son, nor thy daughter, thy manservant, nor thy maidservant, nor thy cattle, nor thy stranger that is within thy gates." KJV*

We are to hallow it.

Hallow means that we are to "set it apart," or make it different from the other days of the week.

Jeremiah 17:22, *"Neither carry forth a burden out of your houses on the sabbath day, neither do ye any work, but hallow ye the sabbath day, as I commanded your fathers." KJV*

Sabbath is a day of rest.

This may be the hardest for you to do. This can be a major battle for me, just to stop to rest.

Exodus 31:15, *"but in the seventh is the sabbath of rest..." KJV*

We are to make the Sabbath holy to YeHoVaH.

This means that we are to set our attention on YeHoVaH that day.

Exodus 31:15, *"...but in the seventh is the sabbath of rest, holy to the LORD:..."KJV*

Exodus 20:11, *"For in six days the LORD made heaven and earth, the sea, and all that in them is, and rested the seventh day: wherefore the LORD blessed the sabbath day, and hallowed it." KJV*

The Sabbath is to be a sign between YeHoVaH and His people. Although YeHoVaH brought the Gentile believers into the kingdom, He has not cast off His people, Israel, or the seventh-day Sabbath.

We are to set the Sabbath apart and make it different from other days of the week.

Exodus 31:17, *"It is a sign between me and the children of Israel for ever: for in six days the LORD made heaven and earth, and on the seventh day he rested, and was refreshed." KJV*

Romans 11:1a, *"I say then, Hath God cast away his people? God forbid." KJV*

Romans 11:17, *"And if some of the branches be broken off, and thou, being a wild olive tree, wert grafted in among them, and with them partakest of the root and fatness of the olive tree;" KJV*

Galatians 3:29, *"And if ye be Christ's [Messiah's], then are ye Abraham's seed, and heirs according to the promise." KJV*

Rest on the Sabbath.

For believers, observing the Sabbath can open the door to experiencing the rest that we find in Yeshua.

Hebrews 4:1-4, 9-11, *"Let us therefore fear, lest, a promise being left us of entering into his rest, any of you should seem to come short of it. For unto us was the gospel preached, as well as unto them: but the word preached did not profit them, not being mixed with faith in them that heard it. For we which have believed do enter into rest, as he said, As I have sworn in my wrath, if they shall enter into my rest: although the works were finished from the foundation of the world. For he spake in a certain place of the seventh day on this wise, And God did rest the seventh day from all his works...There remaineth therefore a rest to the people of God. For he that is entered*

79

into his rest, he also hath ceased from his own works, as God did from his. Let us labour therefore to enter into that rest, lest any man fall after the same example of unbelief." KJV

We are to bear no burden or kindle a fire.

Jeremiah 17:27a, *"But if ye will not hearken unto me to hallow the sabbath day, and not to bear a burden, even entering in at the gates of Jerusalem on the sabbath day;" KJV*

Numbers 15:32-36, *"And while the children of Israel were in the wilderness, they found a man that gathered sticks upon the sabbath day. And they that found him gathering sticks brought him unto Moses and Aaron, and unto all the congregation. And they put him in ward, because it was not declared what should be done to him. And the LORD said unto Moses, The man shall be surely put to death: all the congregation shall stone him with stones without the camp. And all the congregation brought him without the camp, and stoned him with stones, and he died; as the LORD commanded Moses." KJV*

The verses from Numbers are referring to labor; the process of gathering wood and preparing a fire for cooking.

We are to reverence YeHoVaH's sanctuary on the Sabbath.

Leviticus 26:2, *"Ye shall keep my sabbaths, and reverence my sanctuary: I am the LORD." KJV*

The term, "Sabbaths" is used in the context of the weekly and yearly Sabbaths.

From a New Testament view, the body of the believer is the temple of God.

I Corinthians 6:19, *"What? know ye not that your body is the temple of the Holy Ghost which is in you, which ye have of God, and ye are not your own?" KJV*

We are to assemble for teaching, ministering, worship, and prayer on the Sabbath.

Leviticus 23:3, *"Six days shall work be done: but the seventh day is the sabbath of rest, an holy convocation; ye shall do no work therein: it is the sabbath of the LORD in all your dwellings." KJV*

The term "convocation" (Hebrew "miqra"), means "something called out," "a public meeting," "a rehearsal," "an assembly," or "a sacred gathering"; possibly for a reading.

Hebrews 10:25, *"Not forsaking the assembling of ourselves together, as the manner of some is; but exhorting one another: and so much the more, as ye see the day approaching." KJV*

Jeremiah 17:26, *"And they shall come from the cities of Judah, and from the places about Jerusalem, and from the land of Benjamin, and from the plain, and from the mountains, and from the south, bringing burnt offerings, and sacrifices, and meat offerings, and incense, and bringing sacrifices of praise, unto the house of the LORD." KJV*

Yeshua as well as Paul observed the Sabbath.

Mark 6:2, *"And when the sabbath day was come, he began to teach in the synagogue: and many hearing him were astonished, saying, from whence hath this man these things? And what wisdom is this which is given unto him, that even such mighty works are wrought by his hands?" KJV*

Acts 17:2, *"And Paul, as his manner was, went in unto them, and three sabbath days reasoned with them out of the scriptures," KJV*

Paul prayed with believers on the Sabbath.

Acts 16:13, *"And on the sabbath we went out of the city by a river side, where prayer was wont to be made; and we sat down, and spake unto the women which resorted thither."* KJV

We may keep the Sabbath by doing good.

Yeshua responded to the question about doing good by saying:

Matthew 12:11-12, *"And he said unto them, What man shall there be among you, that shall have one sheep, and if it fall into a pit on the sabbath day, will he not lay hold on it, and lift it out? How much then is a man better than a sheep?* ***Wherefore it is lawful to do well on the sabbath days.***" *KJV*

Yeshua healed on the Sabbath.

John 9:14, *"And it was the sabbath day when Jesus [Yeshua] made the clay, and opened his eyes."* KJV

We are to avoid extensive travel on the Sabbath.

Matthew 24:20, *"But pray ye that your flight be not in the winter, neither on the sabbath day."* KJV

One was permitted only to travel a short distance, because of the stress exerted in travel.

Acts 1:12, *"Then returned they unto Jerusalem from the mount called Olivet, which is from Jerusalem a sabbath day's journey."* KJV

Exodus 16:29, *"See, for that the* LORD *hath given you the sabbath, therefore he giveth you on the sixth day the bread of two days; abide ye every man in his place, let no man go out of his place on the seventh day."* KJV

Again, we should understand that travel in Biblical times was often by foot and exhausting.

We are not to buy or sell on the Sabbath.

Nehemiah 10:31, *"And if the people of the land bring ware or any victuals on the sabbath day to sell, that we would not buy it of them on the sabbath, or on the holy day:" KJV*

Is it not strange that internationally, Saturday is usually the biggest "sales" day? Some believers even have their garage sales on Saturday.

We are to avoid doing our own pleasure or speaking our own words on the Sabbath.

Isaiah 58:13-14, *"If you hold back your foot on Shabbat from pursuing your own interests on my holy day; if you call Shabbat a delight, ADONAI'S [YEHOVAH'S] holy day, worth honoring; then honor it by not doing your usual things or pursuing your interests or speaking about them. If you do, you will find delight in ADONAI [YEHOVAH] — I will make you ride on the heights of the land and feed you with the heritage of your ancestor Ya'akov, for the mouth of ADONAI [YEHOVAH] has spoken." CJB*

We are to redirect our attention from what we want to do or say and focus on what YeHoVaH wants from us. It is not to be a day of entertainment. Isn't it strange that most major sporting events are held Friday nights and Saturday? Have you ever set aside the Sabbath just to think about the things of YeHoVaH?

We are to call the Sabbath a delight.

Isaiah 58:13, *"...and call the sabbath a delight..." KJV*

In other words, we are to look forward to the Sabbath and purpose to enjoy it. Once we start it, we will look forward to the rest and time with our Heavenly Father.

Exodus 31:16, *"The people of Isra'el are to keep the Shabbat, to observe Shabbat through all their generations as a perpetual covenant."* CJB

The Sabbath is a time to celebrate the covenant we have with the Father.

Isaiah 58:14, *"Then shalt thou delight thyself in the LORD;"* KJV

YeHoVaH is to be the center of the Sabbath. We should seek to do HIS pleasure.

We may carry out basic necessities on the Sabbath.

Matthew 12:1-5, *"At that time Yeshua went on the sabbath day through the corn; and his disciples were an hungered, and began to pluck the ears of corn, and to eat. But when the Pharisees saw it, they said unto him, Behold, thy disciples do that which is not lawful to do upon the sabbath day. But he said unto them, Have ye not read what David did, when he was an hungered, and they that were with him; How he entered into the house of God, and did eat the shewbread, which was not lawful for him to eat, neither for them which were with him, but only for the priests? Or have ye not read in the [Law/Torah], how that on the sabbath days the priests in the temple profane the sabbath, and are blameless?"* KJV

How Yeshua observed the Sabbath.

Luke 4:16-20, *"And he came to Nazareth, where he had been brought up: and, as his custom was, he went into the synagogue on the sabbath day, and stood up for to read. And there was delivered unto him the book of the prophet Esaias.*

And when he had opened the book, he found the place where it was written, The Spirit of the Lord is upon me, because he hath anointed me to preach the gospel to the poor; he hath sent me to heal the brokenhearted, to preach deliverance to the captives, and recovering of sight to the blind, to set at liberty them that are bruised, To preach the acceptable year of the Lord. And he closed the book, and he gave it again to the minister, and sat down. And the eyes of all them that were in the synagogue were fastened on him." KJV

Yeshua read aloud the Scriptures. However, look at what he read.

- *Anointing of the Spirit and then the purposes of the anointing*
- *Preaching the good news to the poor*
- *Healing the brokenhearted*
- *Delivering the captives*
- *Recovering of sight to the blind (physical and spiritual)*
- *Setting free those who are emotionally bruised*
- *Proclaiming the acceptable year of the Lord*

What did Yeshua do on the Sabbath? He taught and he healed. He delivered the man with an unclean spirit; and He went to Simon's house and healed Simon's mother-in-law.

Luke 4:31-39, *"And came down to Capernaum, a city of Galilee, and taught them on the sabbath days. And they were astonished at his doctrine: for his word was with power. And in the synagogue there was a man, which had a spirit of an unclean devil, and cried out with a loud voice, Saying, Let us alone; what have we to do with thee, thou Jesus [Yeshua] of Nazareth? Art thou come to destroy us? I know thee who thou art; the Holy One of God. And Jesus [Yeshua] rebuked him, saying, Hold thy peace, and come out of him. And when the devil had thrown him in the midst, he came out of him, and hurt him not. And they were all amazed, and spake among themselves, saying, what a word is this! for with authority and power he commandeth the unclean spirits, and they come out.*

85

And the fame of him went out into every place of the country round about. And he arose out of the synagogue, and entered into Simon's house. And Simon's wife's mother was taken with a great fever; and they besought him for her. And he stood over her, and rebuked the fever; and it left her: and immediately she arose and ministered unto them." KJV

Yeshua discipled his followers and taught on the Sabbath.

Luke 6:1-5, "And it came to pass on the second sabbath after the first, that he went through the corn fields; and his disciples plucked the ears of corn, and did eat, rubbing them in their hands. And certain of the Pharisees said unto them, why do ye that which is not lawful to do on the sabbath days? And Jesus [Yeshua] answering them said, Have ye not read so much as this, what David did, when himself was an hungered, and they which were with him; How he went into the house of God, and did take and eat the shewbread, and gave also to them that were with him; which it is not lawful to eat but for the priests alone? And he said unto them, that the Son of man is Lord also of the sabbath." KJV

What else did Yeshua do on the Sabbath?

- He went to the synagogue and taught.
- He healed a man with a withered hand.
- He taught about doing good and ministered to those in need.

Yeshua taught about laying aside our programs, works, and projects.

He came under attack because of what he did and what He taught.

Luke 6:6-11, "And it came to pass also on another sabbath, that he entered into the synagogue and taught: and there was a man whose right hand was withered. And the scribes and Pharisees watched him, whether he would heal on the sabbath day; that they might find an accusation against him. But he knew their thoughts, and said to the man, which had the withered hand, rise up, and stand forth in the midst. And he arose and stood forth. Then said Yeshua unto them, I will ask you one thing; Is it lawful on the sabbath days to do good, or to do evil? to save life, or to destroy it? And looking round about upon them all, he said unto the man, Stretch forth thy hand. And he did so: and his hand was restored whole as the other. And they were filled with madness; and communed one with another what they might do to Yeshua." KJV

Luke 13:10-17, "And he was teaching in one of the synagogues on the sabbath. And, behold, there was a woman, which had a spirit of infirmity eighteen years, and was bowed together, and could in no wise lift up herself. And when Yeshua saw her, he called her to him, and said unto her, Woman, thou art loosed from thine infirmity. And he laid his hands on her: and immediately she was made straight, and glorified God. And the ruler of the synagogue answered with indignation, because that Yeshua had healed on the sabbath day, and said unto the people, There are six days in which men ought to work: in them therefore come and be healed, and not on the sabbath day. The Lord then answered him, and said, Thou hypocrite, doth not each one of you on the sabbath loose his ox or his ass from the stall, and lead him away to watering? And ought not this woman, being a daughter of Abraham, whom Satan hath bound, lo, these eighteen years, be loosed from this bond on the sabbath day? And when he had said these things, all his adversaries were ashamed: and all the people rejoiced for all the glorious things that were done by him." KJV

Yeshua taught on the Sabbath. He healed the woman with an infirmity, and taught about ministering to those in need on the Sabbath. Why did He do it on the Sabbath? Possibly this was meant to demonstrate to the priests and rulers of the synagogue what YeHoVaH wanted to do for His people when they gathered in His presence. He met the immediate needs of people, and also set a pattern for the ministry. I believe that if we set aside the

Sabbath to minister, we will be less likely to miss opportunities to minister during the week.

He was teaching that ministering on the Sabbath causes a miraculous growth in the kingdom that would apply to the Messianic Communities as well.

Luke 13:18-21, *"Then said he, 'Unto what is the kingdom of God like? And whereunto shall I resemble it? It is like a grain of mustard seed, which a man took, and cast into his garden; and it grew, and waxed a great tree; and the fowls of the air lodged in the branches of it.' And again he said, 'Whereunto shall I liken the kingdom of God? It is like leaven, which a woman took and hid in three measures of meal, till the whole was leavened.'" KJV*

Additional verses below, describe when Yeshua fellowshipped with a leader of the Synagogue and taught about healing on the Sabbath.

Luke 14:1-6, *"And it came to pass, as he went into the house of one of the chief Pharisees to eat bread on the sabbath day, that they watched him. And, behold, there was a certain man before him which had the dropsy. And Jesus [Yeshua] answering spake unto the lawyers and Pharisees, saying, 'Is it lawful to heal on the sabbath day?' And they held their peace. And he took him, and healed him, and let him go; and answered them, saying, 'which of you shall have an ass or an ox fallen into a pit, and will not straightway pull him out on the sabbath day?' And they could not answer him again to these things." KJV*

Luke 14:7-11, *"And he put forth a parable to those which were bidden, then he marked how they chose out the chief rooms; saying unto them, 'When thou art bidden of any man to a wedding, sit not down in the highest room; lest a more honourable man than thou be bidden of him; And he that bade thee and him come and say to thee, Give this man place; and thou begin with shame to take the lowest room. But when thou*

art bidden, go and sit down in the lowest room; that when he that bade thee cometh, he may say unto thee, Friend, go up higher: then shalt thou have worship in the presence of them that sit at meat with thee. For whosoever exalteth himself shall be abased; and he that humbleth himself shall be exalted.'"
KJV

Yeshua taught about humility – placing the needs of others before ourselves. He humbled himself by often mingling with the people to demonstrate common social courtesy, and as a way to teach them.

Luke 14:12-14, *"Then said he also to him that bade him, 'When thou makest a dinner or a supper, call not thy friends, nor thy brethren, neither thy kinsmen, nor thy rich neighbours; lest they also bid thee again, and a recompense be made thee. But when thou makest a feast, call the poor, the maimed, the lame, the blind: And thou shalt be blessed; for they cannot recompense thee: for thou shalt be recompensed at the resurrection of the just.'" KJV*

In Luke, Yeshua continues to teach those present. He taught specifically about ministry to the poor, the maimed, the halt and the blind. He may have even implied distributing food. He said to go to the highways and hedges and compel them to come in.

Luke 14:15-24, *"And when one of them that sat at meat with him heard these things, he said unto him, 'Blessed is he that shall eat bread in the kingdom of God.' Then said he unto him, 'A certain man made a great supper, and bade many: And sent his servant at supper time to say to them that were bidden, Come; for all things*

We are to call the sabbath a delight.
Isaiah 58:13

are now ready. And they all with one consent began to make excuse. The first said unto him, I have bought a piece of ground, and I must needs go and see it: I pray thee have me excused. And another said, I have bought five yoke of oxen, and I go to prove them: I pray thee have me excused. And another said, I have married a wife, and therefore I cannot come. So that servant came, and shewed his lord these things. Then the master of the house being angry said to his servant, Go out quickly into the streets and lanes of the city, and bring in hither the poor, and the maimed, and the halt, and the blind. And the servant said, Lord, it is done as thou hast commanded, and yet there is room. And the lord said unto the servant, Go out into the highways and hedges, and compel them to come in, that my house may be filled. For I say unto you, that none of those men which were bidden shall taste of my supper.'" KJV

How Paul observed the Sabbath.

Paul went to the synagogue on the Sabbath. He exhorted the people there by reading and preaching from the Word.

Acts 13:14-16, "But when they departed from Perga, they came to Antioch in Pisidia, and went into the synagogue on the sabbath day, and sat down. And after the reading of the law [Torah] and the prophets the rulers of the synagogue sent unto them, saying, 'Ye men and brethren, if ye have any word of exhortation for the people, say on.' Then Paul stood up, and beckoning with his hand said, 'Men of Israel, and ye that fear God, give audience.'" KJV

The above passage continues by saying that the Gentiles asked him to preach the next Sabbath. The following Sabbath, almost the whole city came together to hear Paul's preaching (*Acts 13:41-44*).

On another occasion Paul joined a prayer meeting. He witnessed, reasoned with them from the Scriptures, and baptized.

Acts 16:13-15, "And on the sabbath we went out of the city by a river side, where prayer was wont to be made; and we sat down, and spake unto the women which resorted thither. And a certain woman named Lydia, a seller of purple, of the city of Thyatira, which worshipped God, heard us: whose heart the Lord opened, that she attended unto the things which were spoken of Paul. And when she was baptized, and her household, she besought us, saying, 'If ye have judged me to be faithful to the Lord, come into my house, and abide there.' And she constrained us." KJV

On other occasions, Paul reasoned with both Jews and Greeks from the Scriptures.

***Acts 17:2**, "And Paul, as his manner was, went in unto them, and three sabbath days reasoned with them out of the scriptures." KJV*

***Acts 18:4**, "And he reasoned in the synagogue every sabbath, and persuaded the Jews and the Greeks." KJV*

How the early Messianic Communities observed the Sabbath.

In the early Messianic Communities, the Jews and Gentiles worshipped together each and every Sabbath. They read from the Law/Torah and the Prophets, as well as had corporate prayer.

***Acts 13:13-16**, "Now when Paul and his company loosed from Paphos, they came to Perga in Pamphylia: and John departing from them returned to Jerusalem. But when they departed from Perga, they came to Antioch in Pisidia, and went into the synagogue on the sabbath day, and sat down. And after the reading of the law [Torah] and the prophets the rulers of the synagogue sent unto them, saying, 'Ye men and brethren, if ye have any word of exhortation for the people, say on.' Then Paul stood up, and beckoning with his hand said, 'Men of Israel, and ye that fear God, give audience.'" KJV*

Acts13:42-44, *"And when the Jews were gone out of the synagogue, the Gentiles besought that these words might be preached to them the next sabbath. Now when the congregation was broken up, many of the Jews and religious proselytes followed Paul and Barnabas: who, speaking to them, persuaded them to continue in the grace of God. And the next sabbath day came almost the whole city together to hear the word of God." KJV*

Acts 16:13, *"And on the sabbath we went out of the city by a river side, where prayer was wont to be made; and we sat down, and spake unto the women which resorted thither." KJV*

Acts 17:2-4, *"And Paul, as his manner was, went in unto them, and three sabbath days reasoned with them out of the scriptures, Opening and alleging, that Christ [Messiah] must needs have suffered, and risen again from the dead; and that this Jesus [Yeshua], whom I preach unto you, is Christ [Messiah]. And some of them believed, and consorted with Paul and Silas; and of the devout Greeks a great multitude, and of the chief women not a few." KJV*

Acts 18:4, *"And he reasoned in the synagogue every sabbath, and persuaded the Jews and the Greeks." KJV*

Summary: Observing the Sabbath.

The Sabbath is not a day for languishing around the house doing nothing. It is a day for corporate gathering with believers and for fellowship. Following the examples of Yeshua and Paul, the Sabbath is a day of rest from regular strenuous labor.

- *Spend some time in prayer, alone or with other believers.*
- *Take time to read the Word aloud for personal edification and teaching your family.*
- *Participate in a public worship service.*
- *Fellowship with other believers.*
- *Find someone to disciple in the Lord.*
- *Minister to those in the hospital or nursing homes.*

- *Witness to the lost.*

> **Paul went to the synagogue on the Sabbath.
> The Gentiles there asked him to preach
> the following Sabbath.**
> From Acts 13:42-44

Additional Suggested Applications.

Shabbat is meant to be a celebration of rest. The congregation holds a holy convocation focusing their thoughts on YeHoVaH and exalting His name. One of the highlights of the day is a joyful feast while the community pays total respect to the Most High.

> *Isn't it strange that Saturday is usually one of the biggest sales days in many businesses?*

Unlike pagan festivals, the feasting does not aim at satisfying selfish desires. Even children should know that there should be a balance between their playfulness and their reverence for YeHoVaH and His Sabbath.

There should not be fasting on Shabbat unless it is an extended fast which goes longer than a week. There is to be no regular mundane work on the Shabbat, especially building or creating with the hands. With certain emergency exceptions, building a fire, doing commerce, seeking out worldly entertainment, and doing any activity that causes a fuss, a ruckus, or disrespectfully loud noises are forbidden on the Sabbath. Work that pertains to ministering to the physical and spiritual needs of others is permitted.

Exceptions are allowed when it comes to military and emergency tasks. In such cases, God expects us to use our discretion. He also knows that in a non-Shabbat honoring world, believers are sometimes called to duty on Shabbat. The Sabbath keeper should make every effort not to work on the seventh day by respectfully communicating his wishes to the employer and/or seeking alternative employment. A person who cannot avoid regular work on the Shabbat should definitely seek the Most High for a solution.

> *Spend time in prayer, maybe have a prayer meeting with others.*

On Shabbat there should be praying, praising, worshiping, reading Holy Scriptures, singing unto YeHoVaH, even dancing unto YeHoVaH, and talking to others about YeHoVaH and His Word; that is, whatever honors the Most High.

Remember that the seventh day is sundown Friday to sundown Saturday because "the evening and the morning" separate each day; not sunrise or 12:00 midnight.

Chapter Ten

THE MESSIAH IN THE SABBATH

"For the Son of man is Lord even of the sabbath day."
Matthew 12:8

When we observe the Sabbath, we enter into the rest Yeshua came to provide to all who come and learn of Him.

Matthew11:28–12:8, *"Come unto me, all ye that labour and are heavy laden, and I will give you rest. Take my yoke upon you, and learn of me; for I am meek and lowly in heart: and ye shall find rest unto your souls. For my yoke is easy, and my burden is light. At that time Jesus [Yeshua] went through the grainfields on the Sabbath. His disciples were hungry and began to pick some heads of grain and eat them. When the Pharisees saw this, they said to him, "Look! Your disciples are doing what is unlawful on the Sabbath." He answered, "Haven't you read what David did when he and his companions were hungry? He entered the house of God, and he and his companions ate the consecrated bread—which was not lawful for them to do, but only for the priests. Or haven't you read in the Law that on the Sabbath the priests in the temple desecrate the day and yet are innocent? I tell you that one greater than the temple is here. If you had known what these words mean, 'I desire mercy, not sacrifice,' you would not have condemned the innocent. For the Son of Man is Lord of the Sabbath." KJV*

When we observe the Sabbath, we are to commemorate the rest, which we receive through the finished work of Messiah Yeshua.

Hebrews 4:4, 8-10, *"For He has spoken in a certain place of the seventh day in this way: 'And God rested on the seventh day from all His works;'... For if Joshua had given them rest, then He would not afterward have spoken of another day. There remains therefore a rest for the people of God. For he who has entered His rest has himself also ceased from his works as God did from His." NKJV*

Yeshua fulfilled the works of the Law/Torah that through faith we might enter into his rest.

***Hebrews 4:11**, "Let us labour [be diligent] therefore to enter into that rest, lest any man fall after the same example of unbelief." KJV*

The writer of Hebrews uses this oxymoron to highlight the significance of rest as the ultimate expression of faith. To make his point, he cites an incident where the congregation of Israel did not believe that God was with them at the waters of Meribah and strove with Moses, and in essence they strove with YeHoVaH. Their attitude reflected their inability to rest in YeHoVaH's ability to deliver them.

"For he that is entered into his rest, he also hath ceased from his own works, as God did from His."
Hebrews 4:10

***Numbers 20:10,11** "And Moses and Aaron gathered the congregation together before the rock, and he said unto them, Hear now, ye rebels; must we fetch you water out of this rock? And Moses lifted up his hand, and with his rod he smote the rock twice: and the water came out abundantly, and the congregation drank, and their beasts also."*

Paul informs us that the rock was Messiah.

***1st Corinthians 10:1-4** "Moreover, brethren, I would not that ye should be ignorant, how that all our fathers were under the cloud, and all passed through the sea; And were all baptized unto Moses in the cloud and in the sea; And did all eat the same spiritual meat; And did all drink the same spiritual drink: for they drank of that spiritual Rock that followed them: and that Rock was Christ."*

Chapter Eleven

BENEFITS OF THE SABBATH

"Then shalt thou delight thyself in the LORD; and I will cause thee to ride upon the high places of the earth, and feed thee with the heritage of Jacob thy father: for the mouth of the LORD hath spoken it."
Isaiah 58:14

The Sabbath is for our benefit.

If it is for us; it is certainly for our benefit.

Mark 2:27, *"And he said unto them, The sabbath was made for man, and not man for the sabbath." KJV*

We understand that observing the Sabbath carried very significant benefits as stated in Leviticus.

Leviticus 26:2-12, *"Ye shall keep my sabbaths, and reverence my sanctuary: I am the LORD. If ye walk in my statutes, and keep my commandments, and do them; Then I will give you rain in due season, and the land shall yield her increase, and the trees of the field shall yield their fruit. And your threshing shall reach unto the vintage, and the vintage shall reach unto the sowing time: and ye shall eat your bread to the full, and dwell in your land safely.* **"and ye shall eat your bread to the full, and dwell in your land safely."** Leviticus 26:5 *And I will give peace in the land, and ye shall lie down, and none shall make you afraid: and I will rid evil beasts out of the land, neither shall the sword go through your land. And ye shall chase your enemies, and they shall fall before you by the sword. And five of you shall chase an hundred, and an hundred of you shall put ten thousand to flight: and your enemies shall fall before you by the sword. For I will have respect unto you, and make you fruitful, and multiply you, and establish my covenant with you. And ye shall eat old store, and*

97

bring forth the old because of the new. And I will set my tabernacle among you: and my soul shall not abhor you. And I will walk among you, and will be your God, and ye shall be my people. KJV

The benefits mentioned above are:

- *Rain in due season*
- *Increase of the harvest*
- *Peace in the land*
- *Land rid of wild beasts*
- *Enemies chased out before us*

And:

- *He would establish His covenant with us.*
- *He would set His tabernacle in our midst (we will know His presence).*
- *We would become fruitful and multiply.*
- *We would have abundance of both the old grain and the new.*
- *He would walk in our midst.*
- *He would accept us.*
- *He would be our God and we would be His people.*

The benefits according to Isaiah are:

Isaiah 58:13-14, "If thou turn away thy foot from the sabbath, from doing thy pleasure on my holy day; and call the sabbath a delight, the holy of the LORD, honourable; and shalt honour him, not doing thine own ways, nor finding thine own pleasure, nor speaking thine own words: Then shalt thou delight thyself in the LORD; and I will cause thee to ride upon the high places of the earth, and feed thee with the heritage of Jacob thy father: for the mouth of the LORD hath spoken it." KJV

Notice that YeHoVaH will cause us to ride upon the high places of the earth (place of honor or respect).

He will also feed us with the heritage of Jacob (fruitfulness and prosperity).

The benefits according to Jeremiah are:

Spend time in prayer, maybe have a prayer meeting with others.

Jeremiah 17:24-26, *"And it shall come to pass, if ye diligently hearken unto me, saith the LORD, to bring in no burden through the gates of this city on the sabbath day, but hallow the sabbath day, to do no work therein; Then shall there enter into the gates of this city kings and princes sitting upon the throne of David, riding in chariots and on horses, they, and their princes, the men of Judah, and the inhabitants of Jerusalem: and this city shall remain for ever. And they shall come from the cities of Judah, and from the places about Jerusalem, and from the land of Benjamin, and from the plain, and from the mountains, and from the south, bringing burnt offerings, and sacrifices, and meat offerings, and incense, and bringing sacrifices of praise, unto the house of the LORD." KJV*

These verses of Jeremiah tell us that we will be brought before royalty and God will bring people to worship with us.

YeHoVaH will bless us when we observe the Sabbath.

Isaiah 56:2, *"Blessed is the man that doeth this, and the son of man that layeth hold on it; that keepeth the sabbath from polluting it, and keepeth his hand from doing any evil." KJV*

"Bless" means to invoke divine care for, and to confer prosperity or happiness upon.

My personal benefits

From personal experience, I greatly look forward to each Sabbath as a day of rest from the activities of daily living. It is a time to relax; focus my attention on YeHoVaH, spend time in the Word, worship, and receive a spiritual renewal. This also revives me mentally, emotionally, and physically. I now have a greater zest for life. The Sabbath is also an opportunity for my family and I to spend some quality time together. Instead of running from place to place and each of us going in our own direction, we all come together and spend time with each other in a settled atmosphere.

The Sabbath is for our rest.

Many times we just wear ourselves out because we don't get the rest we need. My advice to some of my clients is to go home and get some rest. Then, we can begin counseling.

Exodus 31:15,"...but in the seventh is the sabbath of rest,..."
KJV

The Sabbath brings us refreshment.

Exodus 31:17, "...for in six days the LORD made heaven and earth, and on the seventh day he rested, and was refreshed."
KJV

If God was refreshed when he rested on the seventh day, observing the Sabbath should also refresh us.

We receive revelation from God.

100

When we observe the Sabbath, we place ourselves in a position to receive revelation from God as exemplified by the letters sent to the Messianic communities mentioned in The Book of Revelation.

Revelation 1:10-11, "I was in the Spirit on the Lord's day, and heard behind me a great voice, as of a trumpet, Saying, 'I am Alpha and Omega, the first and the last: and, What thou seest, write in a book, and send it unto the seven churches which are in Asia; unto Ephesus, and unto Smyrna, and unto Pergamos, and unto Thyatira, and unto Sardis, and unto Philadelphia, and unto Laodicea.'" KJV

However, we often have to "be still" to hear from God.

Psalms 46:10, "Be still, and know that I am God: I will be exalted among the heathen, I will be exalted in the earth." KJV

We receive healings.

We put ourselves in a position to receive physical health and healing when we observe the Sabbath as a part of the Commandments of YeHoVaH.

> **"Blessed is this man that keepeth the sabbath from polluting it."**
> **Isaiah 56:2,** KJV

Exodus 15:26, "And said, If thou wilt diligently hearken to the voice of the LORD thy God, and wilt do that which is right in his sight, and wilt give ear to his commandments, and keep all his statutes, I will put none of these diseases upon thee, which I have brought upon the Egyptians: for I am the LORD that healeth thee." KJV

Exodus 23:25, "And ye shall serve the LORD your God, and he shall bless thy bread, and thy water; and I will take sickness away from the midst of thee." KJV

101

We should understand that the root of all disease is in the breaking of the Commandments of God.

> ***Deuteronomy 28:15***, *"But it shall come to pass, if thou wilt not hearken unto the voice of the LORD thy God, to observe to do all his commandments and his statutes which I command thee this day; that all these curses shall come upon thee, and overtake thee." KJV*

We will be blessed.

When we observe the Sabbath according to God's Commandments, the BLESSINGS of YeHoVaH will overtake us.

> ***Deuteronomy 28:1-2***, *"And it shall come to pass, if thou shalt hearken diligently unto the voice of the LORD thy God, to observe and to do all his commandments which I command thee this day, that the LORD thy God will set thee on high above all nations of the earth. And all these blessings shall come on thee, and overtake thee, if thou shalt hearken unto the voice of the LORD thy God." KJV*

Continuing in verses 3-14, more blessings are stated.

- *We will be blessed wherever we are.*
- *We will become fruitful.*
- *Our business will become prosperous.*
- *We will overcome our enemies.*
- *God will bless whatever we put our hands to do.*
- *We will be set apart unto the LORD.*
- *God will prosper us in goods, family, and harvest.*
- *God will make us the lender, not the borrower.*
- *The LORD will send rain in its season.*
- *God will place us in leadership positions.*

<u>*Salvation is through Yeshua.*</u>

Just keeping the Commandments of God will not save anyone. The Jews relied on works (keeping the Law/Torah) alone as a means for salvation without faith (*Hebrews 4:2*). However, we are saved by grace through faith in Yeshua (a gift of YeHoVaH).

> ***Ephesians 2:8-9***, *"For by grace are ye saved through faith; and that not of yourselves: it is the gift of God. Not of works, lest any man should boast."* KJV

> ***Romans 3:20***, *"Therefore by the deeds of the law [Torah] there shall no flesh be justified in his sight: for by the law [Torah] is the knowledge of sin."* KJV

Attempting to keep the Commandments of God will not save anyone.

> ***Romans 3:28***, *"Therefore we conclude that a man is justified by faith without the deeds of the law [Torah]."* KJV

> ***Romans 3:31***, *"Do we then make void the law [Torah] through faith? Certainly not! On the contrary, we establish the law [Torah]."* NKJV

> ***I Corinthians 6:12***, *"All things are lawful unto me, but all things are not expedient: all things are lawful for me, but I will not be brought under the power of any."* KJV

In summary, James writes on the relationship between faith and works. James also refutes two wrong ways of thinking: we do good works to be saved in order "to go to heaven," as the Christian would say; and we do good works to "keep our salvation."

James 2:14-26, *"What doth it profit, my brethren, though a man say he hath faith, and have not works? can faith save him? If a brother or sister be naked, and destitute of daily food, And one of you say unto them, 'Depart in peace, be ye warmed and filled;' notwithstanding ye give them not those things which are needful to the body; what doth it profit? Even so faith, if it hath not works, is dead, being alone. Yea, a man may say, 'Thou hast faith, and I have works: show me thy faith without thy works, and I will show thee my faith by my works.' Thou believe that there is one God; thou doest well: the devils also believe, and tremble. But wilt thou know, O vain man that faith without works is dead? Was not Abraham our father justified by works, when he had offered Isaac his son upon the altar? Seest thou how faith wrought with his works, and by works was faith made perfect? And the scripture was fulfilled which saith, Abraham believed God, and it was imputed unto him for righteousness: and he was called the Friend of God. Ye see then how that by works a man is justified, and not by faith only. Likewise also was not Rahab the harlot justified by works, when she had received the messengers, and had sent them out another way? For as the body without the spirit is dead, so faith without works is dead also." KJV*

"If Protestants would follow the Bible, they would worship God on the Sabbath Day. In keeping the Sunday they are following a law of the Catholic Church."
Albert Smith
Catholic Chancellor of the Archdiocese of Baltimore

Chapter Twelve

HOW WE CELEBRATE THE SABBATH

"And it shall come to pass, that from one new moon to another, and from one sabbath to another, shall all flesh come to worship before me, saith the LORD."
Isaiah 66:23

Celebrating the Sabbath in your home and sharing a meal together can be a wonderful weekly experience for you, your family, and guests. Although celebrating the Sabbath is a Commandment, it must be remembered that sharing the Sabbath meal together is a tradition.

Since the Sabbath begins at sundown on Friday you must take into consideration how much time you will need to prepare your heart, your home, and your meal. When we extend an invitation to guests to share the Sabbath meal with us, we find out what they like and what they dislike so we don't prepare something they won't enjoy.

Our Sabbath meal includes Challah bread (a traditional twisted egg-bread) which we get from a local bakery, and grape juice or wine. We use grape juice so that all can enjoy it, including the young children.

Before we sit down to share our meal together, everyone is required to wash their hands because we will be passing the bread to one another with our hands once it has been broken. After the food is placed on the table, we sit down to dine. My wife or one of my three daughters (or the woman of your house) will say a blessing to welcome the Sabbath.

The blessing will go something like this:

"Blessed are you YeHoVaH our Father, King of the universe who has commanded us to keep the Sabbath and who calls us to the light, the light of Yeshua the Messiah."

Next is the blessing over the Challah bread. The bread is placed on a decorative plate and usually covered until the time for the blessing. The man of the house takes the bread and says a blessing similar to this:

"Blessed are you YeHoVaH our Father, King of the universe who brings forth bread from the earth."

After the blessing, we break the bread and pass it to the next person, who breaks off a piece and passes it until everyone has a piece. Once everyone has a piece of Challah, we all eat together.

When everyone has been served, we bless the grape juice or wine. Everyone's cup is filled and as the cups are raised, the man of the house pronounces the following blessing:

"Blessed are you YeHoVaH our Father, King of the universe who brings forth the fruit of the vine."

When the blessing is complete, we touch our cups together and greet one another by saying: ***"Shabbat Shalom"*** which means, "Sabbath Peace or Peaceful Sabbath."

Finally we bless/pray for the children before the meal is shared. Usually the father places his hands on the head of each son and says:

"May YeHoVaH make you like Ephraim and Manasseh" *(from Genesis 48:20).*

The blessing for the daughters goes something like this:

"May YeHoVaH make you like Sarah, Rebecca, Rachel and Leah."

The wife is given a blessing by reading from the Book of Proverbs about the virtuous woman, (*Proverbs 31:10-31*).

I lead a prayer of thanksgiving for our meal, and then we share our meal together.

Whenever we have guests in our home on the Sabbath, we will include a prayer/blessing for our guests. The main reason we have guests in our home on the Sabbath is to share with them how to enjoy the gift of the Sabbath given to us by our Heavenly Father. While the world around us is running here and there, we can relax from the day-to-day "busyness" and the burdens of life to enjoy the blessings of the Sabbath and one another.

When the meal is complete, we all retire to the living room to discuss the scriptures. A passage is chosen for reading and then we have a conversation around the scripture passage read.

Because the Sabbath is the day belonging to YeHoVaH, we always try to keep the right attitude and reverential spirit. As much as possible we avoid talking about work, money, or having meaningless discussions. We do our best to keep our conversations God-centered.

Isaiah 58:13-14, "If thou turn away thy foot from the sabbath, from doing thy pleasure on my holy day; and call the sabbath a delight, the holy of the LORD, honourable; and shalt honour

him, not doing thine own ways, nor finding thine own pleasure, nor speaking thine own words: Then shalt thou delight thyself in the LORD; and I will cause thee to ride upon the high places of the earth, and feed thee with the heritage of Jacob thy father: for the mouth of the LORD hath spoken it."
KJV

The next morning we go to worship service together with our brothers and sisters in Messiah. We spend the day together praying, worshipping, singing praises, hearing the Word, giving and receiving ministry, breaking bread, and fellowshipping together.

Returning home as the Sabbath comes to an end (at sundown Saturday evening), we give thanks to our Heavenly Father for the gift of the Sabbath and close the Sabbath with spontaneous prayer from various members of the family. My prayer continues to be:

"Father teach us how to keep your Sabbath day holy in a manner that is pleasing to you. Amen."

SHABBAT SHALOM!

HAS IT BEEN WORTH IT?

*"He that observes the Sabbath aright holds the history of
that which it celebrates to be authentic, and therefore believes
in the creation of the first man; in the creation of a fair abode
for man in the space of six days; in the primeval and absolute
creation of the heavens and the earth, and, as a necessary
antecedent to all this, in the Creator, who at the close of
His latest creative effort, rested on the seventh day."*
James J. Murphy

Much of what we know about religion and going to church on Sunday has been inherited from previous generations. **We do what we know or what we have been taught**. Logic dictates when we know better, or have been taught better, that we do better. Once we have been challenged over what we believe, and have been shown evidence to support what has been presented, one now has to ask oneself, **"Do I continue to believe what I previously believed when I have been shown evidence to the contrary?"**

Although there is a so-called separation of state and church according to the Constitution of the United States of America, religion has had a profound effect on government-created laws which govern its citizens.

At the founding of America, the pilgrims brought a breed of religion similar to the religious thinking of those they were trying to escape. This religious belief was deeply grounded in the observance of Sunday as the day of worship. For the most part, the founding fathers of America acknowledged the "Laws of Nature and of Nature's God*"* from a somewhat skewed viewpoint. They wanted to honor

God in the documents that became known as the *Declaration of Independence* when they declared:

> *"When in the Course of human events, it becomes necessary for one people to dissolve the political bands which have connected them with another, and to assume among the powers of the earth, the separate and equal station to which the Laws of Nature and of Nature's God entitle them, a decent respect to the opinions of mankind requires that they should declare the causes which impel them to the separation.*
>
> *We hold these truths to be self-evident, that all men are created equal, that they are endowed by their Creator with certain unalienable Rights, that among these are Life, Liberty and the pursuit of Happiness."*

It was the choice of words used within the language of the *Declaration of Independence* that caused future generations to make the argument that America is a Christian nation. Along with this identity of being a Christian nation, came all that is associated with Christianity today. Christianity's most notable tenet is Sunday worship.

To further cement Sunday as the day of worship were the Sunday Blue laws, or sabbath laws, which were attempts by some Christians to enforce a traditional Christian Sunday sabbath as a legally mandated day of rest for everyone. Southern and mid-western states also passed numerous laws to protect Sunday during the mid-to-late 19th century. Laws targeted numerous groups including saloon owners, Jews, Seventh-day Adventists, and non-religious peoples. These Sunday laws enacted at the state and local levels would sometimes carry penalties for doing non-religious activities on Sunday as part of an effort to enforce religious observance and church attendance.

Numerous people were arrested for playing cards, baseball, and even fixing wagon wheels on Sunday.

In Texas for example, blue laws prohibited selling house wares such as pots, pans, and washing machines on Sunday until 1985. In Colorado, Illinois, Indiana, Iowa, Louisiana,   Maine, Minnesota, Missouri, Oklahoma, New Jersey, North Dakota, Pennsylvania, and Wisconsin, car dealerships continue to operate under blue-law prohibitions in which an automobile may not be purchased or traded on a Sunday.

Maryland permits Sunday automobile sales only in the counties of Prince George's, Montgomery, and Howard. Similarly, Michigan restricts Sunday sales to only those counties with a population of less than 130,000. Texas and Utah prohibit car dealerships from operating over consecutive weekend days. In some cases these laws were created or retained with the support of those whom they affected; to allow them a day off each week without fear of their competitors still being open.

The rise of the Temperance Movement (When Evangelical preachers of various Christian denominations denounced drinking alcohol as a sin) after the Civil War, led to the passage of many blue laws which forbade the sale of liquor on Sunday whether in a bar or in a retail store. These prohibitions sometimes banned the sale of tobacco products. By the late nineteenth century, certain public entertainments were not allowed on Sunday.

After the failure of Prohibition and the legalization of alcoholic beverages in 1933, many states and localities used their blue laws to prevent the operation of liquor stores and bars on Sunday. Twelve States continue to cling

111

to Prohibition-era Blue Laws banning Sunday liquor sales. These include: Alabama, Indiana, Minnesota, Mississippi, Montana, North Carolina, Oklahoma, South Carolina, Tennessee, Texas, Utah, and West Virginia. Notably, Indiana is the only state in the country that bans beer, wine, and liquor on Sundays.

Many states have repealed Sunday Blue Laws. However numerous counties in the U.S. still have Sunday Blue Laws (e.g., Bergen County, NJ, next to the border of New York State, and 40 Counties in South Carolina). Eight states still have statewide Sunday blue laws. Also outside of the United States, Nova Scotia has voted to retain their blue laws as well as numerous counties in Europe; for example Germany.

Even though Sunday Blue Laws have been legally repealed, the minds of many are still operating from a Sunday Blue Law mentality. Several years ago I lived in a neighborhood where it was frowned upon to mow the lawn on Sunday. There are pockets of communities and whole enclaves where un-official Sunday blue laws are still in effect. Societal pressure makes individuals in these pockets and enclaves feel very uneasy when wanting to do laborious work on Sunday.

For centuries, Evangelicals in this country have misquoted, misinterpreted, and misused Biblical passages to further their anti-Messiah, Torah-less messages using whatever means necessary. Ignorant and unlearned Christians have swallowed those errant messages to their own demise; setting them on a hellish path of continual rejection of YeHoVaH's Commands even though the Word of YeHoVaH is clearly in opposition to such evangelical teachings.

Yeshua's warnings to the people of His day ring true for our generation. Yeshua warned His disciples to beware of the leaven (doctrine or teaching) of three groups: the religious leaders called Pharisees, Sadducees, and Herod (the government).

Matthew 16:6-10, "Then [Yeshua] said unto them, 'Take heed and beware of the leaven of the Pharisees and of the Sadducees.' And they reasoned among themselves, saying, 'It is because we have taken no bread.' Which when Jesus perceived, he said unto them, 'O ye of little faith, why reason ye among yourselves, because ye have brought no bread? Do ye not yet understand, neither remember the five loaves of the five thousand, and how many baskets ye took up? Neither the seven loaves of the four thousand, and how many baskets ye took up?'" KJV

Mark 8:15, "And he charged them, saying, 'Take heed, beware of the leaven of the Pharisees, and of the leaven of Herod.'" KJV

In *Matthew 24* as Yeshua was leaving the temple courts, His disciples pointed to the elegance and beauty of the temple Herod built. They were shocked at Yeshua's response as He proceeded to inform them of the coming destruction of this historic and sacred place of Jewish worship. He said not one stone would be left upon another.

Later as they sat upon the Mount of Olives, they asked Yeshua to tell them privately when would this happen and what would be the sign of His return and the end of the world.

Matthew 24:4-14, "And Jesus [Yeshua] answered and said unto them, 'Take heed that no man deceive you. For many shall come in my name, saying, I am Christ[Messiah]; and shall deceive many. And ye shall hear of wars and rumours of wars: see that ye be not troubled: for all these things must

> *come to pass, but the end is not yet. For nation shall rise against nation, and kingdom against kingdom: and there shall be famines, and pestilences, and earthquakes, in divers places. All these are the beginning of sorrows. Then shall they deliver you up to be afflicted, and shall kill you: and ye shall be hated of all nations for my name's sake. And then shall many be offended, and shall betray one another, and shall hate one another. And many false prophets shall rise, and shall deceive many. And because iniquity shall abound, the love of many shall wax cold. But he that shall endure unto the end, the same shall be saved. And this gospel of the kingdom shall be preached in all the world for a witness unto all nations; and then shall the end come.'" KJV*

After Yeshua's resurrection, He appeared to His disciples one last time and gave them these instructions.

> *Matthew 28:18-20, "And Jesus [Yeshua] came and spake unto them, saying, 'All power is given unto me in heaven and in earth. Go ye therefore, and teach all nations, baptizing them in the name of the Father, and of the Son, and of the Holy Ghost: Teaching them to observe all things whatsoever I have commanded you: and, lo, I am with you always, even unto the end of the world. Amen.'" KJV*

Unfortunately this gospel of the kingdom, *"Teaching them to observe all things whatsoever I have commanded you,"* is not being preached to the ends of the earth or to the nations of the world. Instead, another gospel has taken the place of the gospel of the kingdom.

This other gospel is a gospel ABOUT Jesus, and NOT the gospel that Yeshua taught. This gospel about Jesus is about the death, burial, and resurrection. It is an *emotional* gospel that is designed to lead people into making a decision for Christ, and to invite a savior they barely know to come into their heart.

Yeshua came to reconcile mankind to YeHoVaH and His Commandments. The gospel that is being preached in Christianity today is a gospel that rejects the Commandments of YeHoVaH. It is also a gospel that teaches lawlessness, or that the followers of Jesus do not have to keep the Commandments or the Law of YeHoVaH.

The Internet, radio, and television airwaves are filled with this anti-Messiah message of lawlessness. Christian radio and television are filled with ministers, teachers, and even rabbis who teach that people today are no longer obligated to keep the commandments of YeHoVaH. They are not equipping the saints for the work of ministry, nor are they preparing the people of the world for the return of the Messiah. In fact, the Messiah said that:

> *Matthew 5:19, "Whosoever therefore shall break one of these least commandments, and shall teach men so, he shall be called the least in the kingdom of heaven: but whosoever shall do and teach them, the same shall be called great in the kingdom of heaven." KJV*

Yeshua also said:

> *Matthew 7:21-23, "Not every one that saith unto me, 'Lord, Lord,' shall enter into the kingdom of heaven; but he that doeth the will of my Father which is in heaven. Many will say to me in that day, 'Lord, Lord, have we not prophesied in thy name? and in thy name have cast out devils? And in thy name done many wonderful works?' And then will I profess unto them, 'I never knew you: depart from me, ye that work iniquity.'" KJV*

These are words that no one should hear, especially those who call themselves believers. Yet every minister who preaches that Jesus set people free from the Law, are preparing people to hear those awful and condemning words.

It is this kind of leaven/teaching of modern day Pharisees, Sadducees, and government that impacts religious worldviews; and tints the glasses many look though when reading the Bible today. Many people read the Bible with varied denomination lenses. Much of the arguments presented by those of denominational persuasions are based upon belief systems given to them by religious leaders of their denominations rather than having been exacted from their own scriptural studies.

Furthermore, this Sunday Sabbath religious dogma has been thrust upon the nations of the world often by Evangelical Christian Missionaries who propagated this antinomian message (the message that faith and divine grace bring about salvation and that it is therefore not necessary to keep YeHoVaH's laws). Such beliefs are taught to unsuspecting natives who ignorantly believe they are responding to a call of salvation.

Unfortunately individuals in many nations of the world have been duped like many Americans who believe that a Western Jesus delivered them from the Laws of YeHoVaH. They believe in the ushering in of a Sunday Sabbath, or a Sabbath of their choosing as a day of worship and service to God as they see fit. YeHoVaH forbid!

Fortunately for many, this book has exposed the religious systems of belief. It serves as a voice in the wilderness to call the people of YeHoVaH to repent and to return to His Commandments. The evidence presented in this book is verified by scripture in context. It has been proven that at no point in Biblical history did YeHoVaH change the seventh day Sabbath to become Sunday or any other day. So the question is why do you worship on Sunday?

Once we have been challenged over what we believe and have been shown evidence to support what has been presented, one now must ask:

> *"Do I continue to believe what I previously believed when I have been shown evidence to the contrary?"*

When we know better, or have been taught better, we do better.

Now you have a choice. Do you continue down the broad path and continue the traditions of past generations? Or do you follow the instructions of the preacher who said:

> *Ecclesiastes 12:11-14, "The words of the wise are as goads, and as nails fastened by the masters of assemblies, which are given from one shepherd. And further, by these, my son, be admonished: of making many books there is no end; and much study is a weariness of the flesh. Let us hear the conclusion of the whole matter: Fear God, and keep his commandments: for this is the whole duty of man. For God shall bring every work into judgment, with every secret thing, whether it be good, or whether it be evil." KJV*

Appendix A

DENOMINATIONAL STATEMENTS ABOUT THE SABBATH

"Let us hear the conclusion of the whole matter: Fear God, and keep his commandments: for this is the whole duty of man."
Ecclesiastes 12:13

This chapter contains statements from a total of 16 denominations and other reference sources concerning the Sabbath. These statements are evidence that the denominations are quite aware that the Sabbath is on the seventh day, even though they worship on Sunday. How long must the deception persist before the congregations repent and turn to the real Sabbath and YeHoVaH's Torah?

Anglican

"And where are we told in the Scriptures that we are to keep the first day at all? We are commanded to keep the seventh; but we are nowhere commanded to keep the first day." (Isaac Williams, *Plain Sermons on the Catechism*, Rivington, London, 1851, pp. 334, 336.)

Baptist

"To me it seems unaccountable that Jesus, during three years' discussion with His disciples, often conversing with them upon the Sabbath question...never alluded to any transference of the day; also, that during the forty days of His resurrection life, no such thing was intimated...Of course I quite well know that Sunday did come into use in early Christian history...But what a pity that it comes branded with the mark of Paganism, and christened with the name of the sun-god, then adopted and sanctified by the Papal apostasy, and bequeathed as a sacred legacy to

Protestantism." (Dr. E. T. Hiscox, report of his sermon at the Baptist Minister's Convention, *New York Examiner*, November 16, 1893. http://www.cgca.net/pabco/rcapcas.htm, accessed on April 14, 2014.)

"We believe that the Law of God is the eternal and unchangeable rule of His moral government;" (J. M. Pendleton, *Church Manual Designed for the Use of Baptist Churches*, Judson Press, Philadelphia, 1867, Chapter III, Article XII.)

"The first four commandments set forth man's obligations directly toward God...The fourth commandment sets forth God's claim on man's time and thought...Not one of the ten words is of merely racial significance...The Sabbath was established originally (long before Moses) in no special connection with the Hebrews, but as an institution for all mankind, in commemoration of God's rest after the six days of creation. It was designed for all the descendants of Adam." (*Adult Quarterly, Southern Baptist Convention* series, Aug. 15, 1937.)

"There was never any formal or authoritative change from the Jewish seventh-day Sabbath to the Christian first-day observance." (William Owen Carver, *The Lord's Day in Our Day*, p. 49, http://faithgracetorah.net/2013/06/14/truth-or-traditions-sabbath-or-sun-day/, accessed on April 14, 2014.)

Brethren

"With the views of the law and the Sabbath we once held...and which are still held by perhaps the great majority of the most earnest Christians, we confess that we could not answer Adventists. What is more, neither before or since have I heard or read what would conclusively answer an Adventist in his Scriptural contention that the Seventh day is the Sabbath (*Ex. 20:10*). It is not 'one day in seven' as some put it, but 'the seventh day according to the commandment.'" (*Words of Truth and Grace*, p. 281, http://www.sabbathtruth.com/sabbath-history/denominational- statements-on-the-sabbath/id/981/brethren accessed on April 14, 2014.)

Catholic

"The Sunday, as a day of the week set apart for the obligatory public worship of Almighty God, to be sanctified by a suspension of all servile labor, trade, and worldly avocations and by exercises of devotion, is purely a creation of the Catholic Church...not governed by the enactments of the Mosaic Law. It is part and parcel of the system of the Catholic Church," (*The American Catholic Quarterly Review*, Vol. VIII, From January to October 1883, Hardy and Mahony, Philadelphia, 1883, p. 139.)

"If we would consult the Bible *only*, without Tradition, we ought, for instance, still to keep holy the Saturday with the Jews, instead of ..." (Joseph Deharbe, *A Full Catechism of the Catholic Religion*, Eleventh American Edition, Catholic Publication Society Co., New York, 1880, p. 73.)

"Most Christians assume that Sunday is the biblically approved day of worship. The Roman Catholic Church protests that, indeed, it is not. The Roman Catholic Church itself without any Scriptural authority from God transferred Christian worship from the biblical Sabbath (Saturday) to Sunday, by the command of the pagan Roman Emperor Constantine in 325 AD; and that to try to argue that the change was made in the Bible is both dishonest and a denial of Catholic authority. If Protestantism wants to base its teachings only on the Bible, *it should worship on Saturday.*" (*A Sabbath/Sunday Challenge You Have Never Read*, Christian Biblical Church of God, Reprinted 2008.)

"**Question: Which is the Sabbath day?**

Answer: Saturday is the Sabbath day.

Question: Why do we observe Sunday instead of Saturday?

Answer: We observe Sunday instead of Saturday because the Catholic Church, in the Council of Laodicea (A.D. 336), transferred the solemnity from Saturday to Sunday." (Rev. Peter Geiermann, C.S.S.R., *The Convert's Catechism of Catholic Doctrine*, 3rd ed., 1957, p. 50.)

"**Question: How prove you that the Church hath power to command feasts and holydays?**

Answer: By the very act of changing the sabbath into *Sunday*, which Protestants allow of; and therefore they fondly contradict themselves, by keeping *Sunday* strictly, and breaking most other feasts commanded by the same church." (Henry Tuberville, D.D., *The Douay Catechism of 1649*, quoted in *An Abridgment of the Christian Doctrine*, Excelsior Catholic Publishing House, New York, 1833, p. 58.)

"The Church, on the other hand, after changing the day of rest from the Jewish Sabbath, or seventh day of the week, to the first, made the Third Commandment refer to Sunday as the day to be kept holy as the Lord's Day. The

Council of Trent (Sess. VI, can. xix) condemns those who deny that the Ten Commandments are binding on Christians." (John Stapleton, *The Ten Commandments, The Catholic Encyclopedia*, Robert Appleton Company, New York, 1908, Vol. 4.)

"Protestants...deem it their duty to keep the Sunday holy. Why? Because the Catholic church tells them to do so. They have no other reason." (Herman Joseph Heuser, *The American Ecclesiastical Review*, Dolphin Press, 1914, Vol. 50, p. 236.)

"But you may read the Bible from Genesis to Revelation, and you will not find a single line authorizing the sanctification of Sunday. The Scriptures enforce the religious observance of Saturday, a day which we never sanctify." (Archbishop James Gibbons, Archbishop of Baltimore, *The Faith of Our Fathers*, 93rd ed., John Murphy Company, Baltimore, 1917, Chap. VIII.)

"The Church is above the Bible; and this transference of Sabbath observance from Saturday to Sunday is proof positive of that fact. Deny the authority of the Church and you have no adequate or reasonable explanation or justification for the substitution of Sunday for Saturday in the Third – Protestant Fourth – Commandment of God." (*The Catholic Record*, Vol. XLV, *Sabbath Observance*, September 1, 1923, London, Canada, p. 4.)

"But since Saturday, not Sunday, is specified in the Bible, isn't it curious that non-Catholics who profess to take their religion directly from the Bible and not the Church, observe Sunday instead of Saturday? Yes, of course, it is inconsistent; but this change was made about fifteen centuries before Protestantism was born, and by that time the custom was universally observed. They have continued the custom, even though it rests upon the authority of the Catholic Church and not upon an explicit text in the Bible. That observance remains as a reminder of the Mother Church from which the non-Catholic sects broke away – like a boy running away from home but still carrying in his pocket a picture of his mother or a lock of her hair." (John A. O'Brien, *The Faith of Millions*, Our Sunday Visitor, 1963, p. 473.)

"Perhaps the boldest thing, the most revolutionary change the Church ever did, happened in the first century. The holy day, the Sabbath, was changed from Saturday to Sunday. "The Day of the Lord" (dies Dominica) was chosen, not from any directions noted in the Scriptures, but from the Church's sense of its own power. The day of resurrection, the day of Pentecost, fifty days later, came on the first day of the week. So this would be the new Sabbath. People who think that the Scriptures should be the sole authority, should logically become 7th day Adventists, and keep Saturday holy." (Fr. Leo. Broderick, *Sentinel*, *Pastor's Page*, Saint Catherine Catholic Church, Algonac, Michigan, May 21, 1995, Volume 50, No. 22.)

"...the observance of Sunday by the Protestants is homage they pay, in spite of themselves, to the authority of the [Catholic] Church." (Monsignor Louis Gaston de Segur, *Plain Talk about the Protestantism of To-day*, Donahoe, Boston, 1868, p. 225.)

"[What Important Question Does the Papacy Ask Protestants?] You will tell me that Saturday was the *Jewish* Sabbath, but that the *Christian* Sabbath has been changed to Sunday. Changed! But by whom? Who has authority to change an express commandment of Almighty God? When

God has spoken and said, Thou shalt keep holy the seventh day, who shall dare to say, Nay, thou mayest work and do all manner of worldly business on the seventh day; but thou shalt keep holy the first day in its stead? This is a most important question, which I know not how you can answer.

You are a Protestant, and you profess to go by the Bible and the Bible only; and yet in so important a matter as the observance of one day in seven as a holy day, you go against the plain letter of the Bible, and put another day in the place of that day which the Bible has commanded. The command to keep holy the seventh day is one of the ten commandments; you believe that the other nine are still binding; who gave you authority to tamper with the fourth? If you are consistent with your own principles, if you really follow the Bible and the Bible only, you ought to be able to produce some portion of the New Testament in which this fourth commandment is expressly altered, or at least from which you may confidently infer that it was the will of God that Christians should make that change in its observance which you have made." (Brotherhood of St. Vincent of Paul, *The Clifton Tracts, Vol. III, Why Don't You Keep Holy the Sabbath-Day?*, Burns and Lambert, London, 1852, pp. 3-4.)

"I have repeatedly offered $1000 to anyone who can prove to me from the Bible alone that I am bound to keep Sunday holy. There is no such law in the Bible. It is a law of the holy Catholic Church alone. The Bible says 'Remember that thou keep holy the Sabbath day.' The Catholic Church says, 'No, by my divine power I abolish the Sabbath day and command you to keep holy the first day of the week.' And lo! The entire civilized world bows down in reverent obedience to the commandment of the holy Catholic church... " (T. Enright, Css. R., letter written to *The Colville Examiner*, Saturday, May 8, 1909, Colville, Washington, p. 4.)

"'Tradition, not Scripture,' Lessing says, 'is the rock on which the church of Jesus Christ is built.'" (Adrien Nampon, S.J., *Catholic Doctrine as Defined by the Council of Trent*, Cunningham & Son, Philadelphia, 1869, p. 157.)

"The pope is of so great dignity and so exalted that he is not a mere man...he is as it were God on earth, sole sovereign of the faithful of Christ, chief of kings, having plenitude of power." (Locus Ferraris, *Prompta Bibliotheca*, 1763, Volume VI, Papa II, pp. 25-29.)

"The leader of the Catholic Church is defined by the faith as the Vicar of Jesus Christ (and is accepted as such by believers). The Pope is considered the man on earth who 'takes the place' of the Second Person of the omnipotent God of the Trinity." (John Paul II, *Crossing the Threshold of Hope*, 1994, p. 3.)

" ...pastoral intuition suggested to the Church the christianization of the notion of Sunday as 'the day of the sun,' which was the Roman name for the day and which is retained in some modern languages. (29) This was in order to draw the faithful away from the seduction of cults which worshipped the sun, and to direct the celebration of the day to Christ, humanity's true 'sun.'" (Pope John Paul II, *Dies Domini: Apostolic Letter of the Holy Father Pope John Paul II: on Keeping the Lord's Day Holy: to the Bishops, Clergy and Faithful of the Catholic Church*, Pauline Books and Media, Pennsylvania State University, 1998.)

"The [Catholic] church took the pagan philosophy and made it the buckler of faith against the heathen. She took the pagan, Roman Pantheon, temple of all the gods, and made it sacred to all the martyrs; so it stands to this day. She took the pagan Sunday and made it the Christian Sunday. She took the pagan Easter and made it the feast we celebrate during this season." (William L. Gildea, D.D., *Paschale Gaudium, The Catholic World: A Monthly Magazine of General Literature and Science*, Vol. LVIII, October 1893 to March 1894, The Columbus Press, New York, 1894, p. 809.)

"The retention of the old pagan name of Dies Solis, for Sunday is, in a great measure, owing to the union of pagan and Christian sentiment with which the first day of the week was recommended by Constantine to his subjects – pagan and Christian alike – as the 'venerable' day of the sun." (Arthur P. Stanley, *History of the Eastern Church*, John Murray, 1862, p. 184.)

"From this same Catholic Church you have accepted your Sunday, and that Sunday, as the Lord's day, she has handed down as a tradition; and the entire Protestant world has accepted it as tradition, for you have not an iota of Scripture to establish it." (D. B. Ray, *The Papal Controversy Involving the Claim of the Roman Catholic Church to be the Church of God Between the "American Baptist" and "Church Progress,"* National Baptist Publishing Co., St. Louis, 1892, p. 179.)

"If we consulted the Bible only, we should still have to keep holy the Sabbath Day, that is, Saturday, with the Jews, instead of Sunday;"...(John Laux, M.A., *A Course in Religion for Catholic High Schools and Academies, Part 1*, Benzinger Brothers, New York, 1936, p. 51.)

"The Sabbath was Saturday, not Sunday. The Church altered the observance of the Sabbath to the observance of Sunday. Protestants must be rather puzzled by the keeping of Sunday when God distinctly said, 'Keep holy the Sabbath Day.' The word Sunday does not come anywhere in the Bible, so, without knowing it they are obeying the authority of the Catholic Church." (Canon Henry Taylor Cafferata, *The Catechism Simply Explained*, Burns-Oates & Washbourne, London, 1927, p. 89.)

"Reason and sense demand the acceptance of one or the other of these alternatives: either Protestantism and the keeping holy of Saturday, or Catholicity and the keeping holy of Sunday. Compromise is impossible." (John Cardinal Gibbons, *The Catholic Mirror*, December 23, 1893.)

Church of Christ

"It reversed the Fourth Commandment by doing away with the Sabbath of God's Word, and instituting Sunday as a holiday." (Dr. Nicholas Summerbell, *The History of the Christian Church from its Establishment by Christ to A.D. 1871*, 3rd ed., Office of the Christian Pulpit, Cincinnati, 1873, p. 415.)

Church of England

"At a service commemorating the 400th anniversary of the Church of England prayer book, Archbishopl [sic] Carrington recalled that 'the Bible commandment says on the seventh day thou shalt rest. That is Saturday. Nowhere in the Bible is it laid down that worship should be done on Sunday.' Tradition, he said, had made it a day of worship." (Article from the *Toronto Dialy* [sic] *Star, – Clergy Say*

Tradition Not Bible Ordinance Declared Sunday Holy, Wednesday, October 26, 1949.)

"...I may conclude the fact, which I state to be undeniable, that not any ecclesiastical writer of the first three centuries of the Christian era has attributed the origin of Sunday observance either to an injunction or the example of the Apostles, or to any precept from Christ himself: a fact which is exceedingly strong evidence, that at no time during that period did there exist in the Christian Church any belief or tradition that the religious observance of the Sunday originated in a divine appointment; and, consequently, that the notion of such an origin of the observance must have sprung up among Christians in after times; and is for this reason, in addition to many others before suggested, unworthy of belief." (Sir William Domville, *The Sabbath, or an Examination of the Six Texts Commonly adduced from the New Testtment in Proff of a Christian Sabbath: by a Layman*, Chapman and Hall, London, 1849, p. 307.)

"...the Lord's day did not succeed in the place of the Sabbath...the Lord's day was merely of ecclesiastical institution. It was not introduced by virtue of the fourth commandment, because they for almost three hundred years together kept that day which was in that commandment;...the primitive Christians did all manner of works upon the Lord's day, even in times of persecution, when they are the strictest observers of all the divine commandments; but in this they knew there was none." (Right Rev. Reginald Heber, D.D., *The Whole Works of the Right Rev. Jeremy Taylor D.D.: Ductor Dubitantium*, Spottiswoods and Co., London, 1862, Part I, Book II, Chap. 2, Rule 6. Sections 51 and 59.)

"*Sunday* being the day on which the *Gentiles* solemnly adore *that Planet* and called it *Sunday*, partly from *its* influence on *that day* especially, and partly in respect to its Divine Body (as they conceived it) the Christians thought fit to keep the *same day* and the *same name* of it, that they might not appear causelesly [sic] peevish, and by that means hinder the conversion of the *Gentiles*, and bring a greater prejudice than might be otherwise taken against the *Gospel*." (Thomas Morer, *Discourse in Six Dialogues on the Name, Notion and Observation of the Lord's Day*, Golden Ball, London, 1701, pp. 22-23.)

"The Christian church made no formal, but a gradual and almost unconscious transference of the one day to the other." (F.W. Farrar, D.D., *The Voice From Sinai*, Thomas Whittaker, New York, 1892, p. 167.)

"Take which you will, either of the Fathers, or the Moderns, and we shall find no *Lord's Day* instituted by any *Apostolical Mandate*, no Sabbath set on foot by them upon the *first day of the week*." (Peter Heylyn, *History of the Sabbath*, Henry Seile, London, 1636, p. 410.)

Congregational

"The Christian Sabbath [Sunday] is not in the Scripture, and was not by the primitive [early Christian] church called the Sabbath." (Timothy Dwight, *Theology*, Sermon 107, 1818, Vol. IV, p. 49. Note: Timothy Dwight, 1752-1817, was president of Yale University from 1795-1817.)

"There is no command in the Bible requiring us to observe the first day of the week as the Christian Sabbath."

(Orin Fowler, A.M., *Mode and Subjects of Baptism*, Peirce, Boston, 1835, p. 93.)

Episcopal

"The festival of Sunday, like all other festivals, was always only a human ordinance, and it was far from the intentions of the apostles to establish a divine command in this respect, far from them and from the early apostolic church to transfer the laws of the Sabbath to Sunday." (Dr. Augustus Neander, *History of the Christian Religion and Church During the First Three Centuries*, 2nd ed., Rivington, London, 1842, Vol. I, p. 336.)

Lutheran

"...the observance of the Lord's Day [Sunday] in place of the Sabbath was instituted by the church's authority as a necessary thing are mistaken." (Leif Grane, *Augsburg Confession of Faith: a Commentary*, Augsburg Publishing House, Minneapolis, 1987, p. 247)

"They [the Catholics] allege the Sabbath changed into Sunday, the Lord's Day, contrary to the Decalogue, as it appears, neither is there any example more boasted of than the changing of the Sabbath day. Great, say they, is the power and authority of the church, since it dispensed with one of the Ten Commandments." (Martin Luther, quoted by Christian Heinrich Schott, *Augsburg Confession of Faith*, Ludwig & Co., New York, 1848, p. 171.)

Methodist

"This 'handwriting of ordinances our Lord did blot out, take away, and nail to his cross,' [Colossians 2:14]...

But the moral law contained in the ten commandments, and enforced by the prophets, he did not take away. It was not the design of his coming to revoke any part of this...The moral [law] stands on an entirely different foundation from the ceremonial or ritual law,...Every part of this law must remain in force upon all mankind, and in all ages;" (John Emory, *The Works of the Reverend John Wesley, A. M. in Seven Volumes*, Emory and Waugh, 1831, Vol. 1, pp. 221-222.)

"...no Christian whatsoever is free from the obedience of the commandments which are called moral." (Bishop Andrews, ed., *The Doctrines and Discipline of the Methodist Episcopal Church*, Jennings & Graham, New York, 1904, p. 23.)

"'The Sabbath was made for MAN;' not for the Hebrews, but for all men." (E.O. Haven, *The Pillars of Truth: a Series of Sermons on the Decalogue*, Carlton & Porter, New York, 1866, p. 88.)

"The reason we observe the first day instead of the seventh is based on no positive command. One will search the Scriptures in vain for authority for changing from the seventh day to the first. The early Christians began to worship on the first day of the week because Yeshua rose from the dead on that day. By and by, this day of worship was made also a day of rest, a legal holiday. This took place in the year 321. Our Christian Sabbath, therefore, is not a matter of positive command. It is a gift of the church." (Clovis Gillham Chappell, *Ten Rules for Living*, Cokesbury Press, University of Virginia, 1938, p. 61.)

Moody Bible Institute

"The Sabbath was binding in Eden, and it has been in force ever since. This fourth commandment begins with the word 'remember,' showing that the Sabbath already existed when God wrote the law on the tables of stone at Sinai. How can men claim that this one commandment has been done away with when they will admit that the other nine are still binding?" (D.L. Moody, *Weighed and Wanting: Addresses on the Ten Commandments*, Revell Company, Chicago, 1898.)

"I honestly believe that this commandment [the Fourth or Sabbath commandment] is just as binding today as it ever was. I have talked with men who have said that it has been abrogated, but they have never been able to point to any place in the Bible where God repealed it. When Christ was on earth, He did nothing to set it aside; He freed it from the traces under which the scribes and Pharisees had put it, and gave it its true place. 'The Sabbath was made for man, and not man for the Sabbath.' It is just as practicable and as necessary for men to-day as it ever was-in fact, more than ever, because we live in such an intense age." (D.L. Moody, *Weighed and Wanting: Addresses on the Ten Commandments*, Revell Company, Chicago, 1898.)

Presbyterian

"A further argument for the perpetuity of the Sabbath we have in Matthew xxiv. 20, 'Pray ye that your flight be not in the winter *neither on the Sabbath day.*'... But this final destruction of Jerusalem [AD 68] was after... the Christian dispensation was fully set up. Yet it is plainly implied in these words of our Lord that even then Christians were bound to strict observation of the Sabbath."

(Jonathan Edwards, *The Works of President Edwards in Eight Volumes*, First American Edition, Isaiah Thomas, Worchester, 1809, Vol. VIII, p. 261.)

"We must not imagine that the coming of Christ has freed us from the authority of the law; for it is the eternal rule of a devout and holy life, and must therefore be as unchangeable as the justice of God, which it embraced, is constant and uniform." (*The John Calvin Bible Commentaries: the Harmony of the Gospels*, Extended Annotated Edition, Vol. 1.)

"The moral law doth for ever bind all, as well justified persons as others, to the obedience thereof; and that not only in regard to the matter contained in it, but also in respect of the authority of God the Creator who gave it. Neither doth Christ in the gospel in any way dissolve, but much strengthen this obligation." (*Westminster Confession of Faith*, Chapter 19, Art. 5.)

Southern Baptist

"The sacred name of the Seventh day is Sabbath. This fact is too clear to require argument [Exodus 20:10 quoted]...on this point the plain teaching of the Word has been admitted in all ages...Not once did the disciples apply the Sabbath law to the first day of the week, – that folly was left for a later age, nor did they pretend that the first day supplanted the seventh." (Joseph Hudson Taylor, *The Sabbatical Question*, pp. 14-17, 41.)

Dictionaries and Encyclopedias

"SABBATH...it must be confessed that there is no law in the New Testament concerning the first day." (*Buck's*

Theological Dictionary http://www.takeacopy.com/files/ index.htm, accessed on April 14, 2014.)

"Thus we learn from Socrates (H.E., vi.c.8) that in his time public worship was held in the churches of Constantinople on both days...The view that the Christian's Lord's day or Sunday is but the Christian Sabbath deliberately transferred from the seventh to the first day of the week does not indeed find categorical expression till a much later period...The earliest recognition of the observance of Sunday as a legal duty is a constitution of Constantine in A.D. 321, enacting that all courts of justice, inhabitants of towns, and workshops were to be at rest on Sunday (venerabili die Solis), with an exception in favour of those engaged in agricultural labour...The Council of Laodicea (p. 363)...forbids Christians from judaizing and resting on the Sabbath day, preferring the Lord's day, and so far as possible resting as Christians." (Encyclopedia Britannica, 1899 ed., Vol. XXIII, p. 654.)

"...it must be confessed that there is no law in the New Test. [Testament] concerning the first day." (John McClintock and James Strong, *Cyclopedia of Biblical, Theological, and Ecclesiastical Literature*, Harper & Brothers, New York, 1880, Vol. IX, p. 196.)

"**SUNDAY** (Dies Solis, of the Roman calendar, 'day of the sun,' because dedicated to the sun), the first day of the week, was adopted by the early Christians as a day of worship. The 'sun' of Latin adoration they interpreted as the 'Sun of Righteousness.'...No regulations for its observance are laid down in the New Testament, nor, indeed, is its observance even enjoined;" (Philip Schaff, *A Religious Encyclopedia or Dictionary of Biblical,*

Historical, Doctrinal, and Practical Theology, Funk & Wagnall's, New York, 1891 Edition, Vol. IV, p. 2259.)

"**SABBATH**...As the Sabbath is of divine institution, so it is to be kept holy unto the Lord. Numerous have been the days appointed by men for religious services; but these are not binding, because of human institution. Not so the sabbath. Hence the fourth commandment is ushered in with a peculiar emphasis – '*Remember* that thou keep holy the sabbath day.'...The abolition of it would be unreasonable;" (Charles Buck, *A Theological Dictionary*, 1830 ed., p. 537)

"But although it [Sunday] was in the primitive times indifferently called the Lord's day, or Sunday, yet it was never denominated the Sabbath; a name constantly appropriate to Saturday, or the seventh day, both by sacred and ecclesiastical writers." (Id., p. 572.)

Infidel

Infidel is an unbeliever: somebody who does not believe in a major religion; or a nonbeliever: somebody with no religious belief.

"Probably very few Christians are aware of the fact that what they call the 'Christian Sabbath' (Sunday) is (like almost everything pertaining to Christianity) of pagan origin.

The first observance of Sunday that history records is in the fourth century, when Constantine issued an edict (not requiring its *religious* observance, but simply *abstinence from work*) reading, 'Let all the judges and people of the town *rest* and all the various trades be suspended on the *venerable day of the Sun*.' At the time of the issue of this edict, Constantine was a Sun-worshipper; therefore it could have had no relation whatever to Christianity." (Henry M. Taber, *Faith or Fact*, Eckler, New York, 1897, p. 112.)

"I challenge any priest or minister of the Christian religion to show me the *slightest* authority for the religious observance of Sunday. And, if such cannot be shown by them, why is it that they are constantly preaching about Sunday as a *holy day*...The claim that Sunday takes the place of Saturday, and that because the Jews were supposed to be commanded to keep the *seventh* day of the week holy, *therefore* the *first* day of the week should be so kept by Christians, is so utterly absurd as to be hardly worth considering...That Paul habitually observed and preached on the *seventh* day of the week, is shown in Acts xviii: 4, – 'And he reasoned in the synagogue *every Sabbath*' (Saturday)." (Henry M. Taber, *Faith or Fact*, Eckler, New York, 1897, pp. 114, 116.)

Miscellaneous

"The first precept in the Bible is that of sanctifying the seventh day: 'God blessed the seventh day, and sanctified it.' *Genesis 2:3* This precept was confirmed by God in the Ten Commandments: 'Remember the Sabbath day to keep It holy...The seventh day is the Sabbath of the Lord thy God.' *Exodus 20: 8, 10.* On the other hand, Christ declares that He is not come to destroy the law, but to fulfill it. (*Matthew 5:17.*) He Himself observed the Sabbath: 'And, as His custom was, He went into the synagogue on the Sabbath day.' *Luke 4: r6.* His disciples likewise observed it after His death: 'They...rested the Sabbath day, according to the commandment.' *Luke 23:56.*

Yet with all this weight of Scripture authority for keeping the Sabbath or seventh day holy, Protestants of all denominations make this a profane day and transfer the obligation of it to the first day of the week, or the Sunday. Now what authority had they for doing this? None at all but the unwritten word, or tradition of the Catholic Church, which declares that the apostle made the change in honour of Christ's resurrection, and the descent of the Holy Ghost on that day of the week." (Right Rev. John Milner D.D., *The End of Religious Controversy in a Friendly Correspondence Between a Religious Society of Protestants and a Catholic Divine*, Dunigan and Brother, New York, p. 71.)

"Sabbath means, of course, Saturday, the seventh day of the week, but the early Christians changed the observance to Sunday, to honour the day on which Christ arose from the dead." (Fulton Oursler, Cosmopolitan, Sept. 1951, pp. 34-35.)

"I do not pretend to be even an amateur scholar of the Scriptures. I read the Decalogue merely as an average man searching for guidance, and in the immortal 'Ten Words' I find a blueprint for the good life." (Fulton Oursler, *Cosmopolitan*, Sept. 1951, pp. 34-35.)

"Most certainly the Commandments are needed today, perhaps more than ever before. Their divine message confronts us with a profound moral challenge in an epidemic of evil; a unifying message acceptable alike to Jew, Moslem, and Christian. Who, reading the Ten in the light of history and of current events, can doubt their identity with the eternal law of nature?" (Fulton Oursler, *Cosmopolitan*, Sept. 1951, pp. 34-35.)

"The Sabbath is commanded to be kept on the

seventh day. It could not be kept on any other day. To observe the first day of the week or the fourth is not to observe the Sabbath...It was the last day of the week, after six days of work, that was to be kept holy. The observance of no other day would fulfill the law." (H. J. Flowers, B.A., B.D., *The Permanent Value of the Ten Commandments*, G. Allen & Unwin Ltd, London, 1927, p. 13.)

"He that observes the Sabbath aright holds the history of that which it celebrates to be authentic, and therefore believes in the creation of the first man; in the creation of a fair abode for man in the space of six days; in the primeval and absolute creation of the heavens and the earth, and, as a necessary antecedent to all this, in the Creator, who at the close of His latest creative effort, rested on the seventh day. The Sabbath thus becomes a sign by which the believers in a historical revelation are distinguished from those who have allowed these great facts to fade from their remembrance." (James J Murphy, "*A Critical and Exegetical Commentary on the Book of Exodus*," Comments on Exodus 20:8-11, T and T Clark International, 1866.)

Appendix B

HEBREW NAMES FOR WEEKDAYS

"And he shall speak great words against the most High, and shall wear out the saints of the most High, and think to change times and laws: and they shall be given into his hand until a time and times and the dividing of time."
Daniel 7:25, KJV

In Hebrew except for the Sabbath day, the individual days of the week have no names, just numbers. The middle column in the table below gives the actual transliterated pronunciation of the names. "Yom" is pronounced "Yome". The "Kh" is a guttural sound often spelled "Ch". There is no "Ch" sound in the Hebrew as there is in English. Modern Hebrew however, can create a "Ch" sound by putting an accent mark (`) in front of the Hebrew letter "Khet" (or "Chet"). This is used only in rare cases in order to properly pronounce such words or names as church or Winston Churchill.

Secular Name	Hebrew Name	Hebrew Meaning
Sunday	Yom Reeshone	First Day
Monday	Yom Shaynee	Second Day
Tuesday	Yom Shlee'shee	Third Day
Wednesday	Yom Revee'ee	Fourth Day
Thursday	Yom Khah'mee'she	Fifth Day
Friday	Yom Ha'shee'shee	Sixth Day
Saturday	Shabbat	Rest

Appendix C
ORIGINS OF SECULAR WEEKDAY NAMES

According to Noah Webster's original 1828 American Dictionary of the English Language, secular weekday names have unbiblical origins associated with planets and pagan gods. Webster's Dictionary also has detailed information on the pagan gods and their associated countries.

Origins of Secular Names of the Week

Day Name	Planet Name	God Name	Origin of Name
Sunday 1st Day	Sun	Sun god	This day was anciently dedicated to the sun and its worship.
Monday 2nd Day	Moon	Moon god	This day was sacred to the moon.
Tuesday 3rd Day	Mars	Tiw	The Mars of our ancestors, the deity that presided over combats, strife, and litigation.
Wednesday 4th Day	Mercury	Woden	A deity or chief among the northern nations of Europe.
Thursday 5th Day	Jupiter	Thor	Thor is related to the words meaning thunder, to strike, hit or produce a shock. It also signifies to drive, to push, and to strike.
Friday 6th Day	Venus	Goddess Frigg or Freia	The Venus of the north, a woman.

143

ABOUT THE AUTHOR

"And we beseech you, brethren, to know them which labour among you, and are over you in the Lord, and admonish you; And to esteem them very highly in love for their work's sake. And be at peace among yourselves."

1 Thessalonians 5:12-13

Arthur Bailey, D. Div., lives in Fort Mill, South Carolina with his wife Marvina and five of their eight children. Internationally known; Dr. Arthur Bailey, apostle and modern-day prophet, is an anointed teacher, preacher, and author. He operates in gifts of the Spirit including prophecy, healing, miracles, words of wisdom and knowledge. He has an apostolic gift to activate others to walk and grow in their respective gifting and anointing.

Apostle Bailey currently oversees the House of Israel, a Law/Torah observant and Spirit-filled Hebrew Roots community in Charlotte, North Carolina; and Abundant Life International Ministries in Cagayan De Oro City, the Philippines. Dr. Bailey's ministries span the continents of Africa, Asia, and North America; equipping God's people for the work of ministry and to answer the call of leadership, discipleship, and service.

As he journeys through the scriptures uncovering ancient biblical truths, Arthur provides a unique perspective and insight into the inspired Word of YeHoVaH. Arthur is a lecturer and keynote speaker at colleges, universities, Messianic communities, and Christian churches. He has produced many DVD teaching series and has taught and brought clarity to many controversial and hard-to-understand biblical passages.

Apostle Bailey broadcasts weekly Sabbath services, discipleship classes; as well as a Spirit Filled Living program on television, radio, and the Internet – locally, nationally, and around the world.

To learn more about these ministries, you can visit:

- **ArthurBaileyMinistries.com**

- **HouseofIsrael.us**

- **Messianic.tv**

This book "Sunday Is Not The Sabbath?" is just the beginning of some amazing discoveries hidden in the books, chapters and verses of Scripture. The following pages provide a sample of the revelations contained in YeHoVaH's Word made known in clear, understandable and applicable teachings by Arthur Bailey.

Order some or all of these DVD teachings and I personally guarantee you will hear, learn and grow!

Thank you for reading "Sunday Is Not The Sabbath?"

Arthur Bailey

In this 4-DVD teaching, Arthur Bailey expounds on each blessing; summarizes the 28 Blessings of *Deuteronomy 28,* and identifies what these blessings look like in our day and time. You will learn how these blessings manifest, and the importance of living a Torah Observant Spirit-Filled Life in order to experience the fullness of the "The 28 Blessings of Deuteronomy 28." Approximately 5 hrs.

28 Blessings of Deuteronomy 28   4 DVDs – $45.00

In this exciting teaching you will learn what are considered to be the Firstfruits Offerings; when they are to be presented, and why Firstfruits Offerings are so important! You will also learn the prayer that is recited during this vital offering which assures the blessing of prosperity upon those who present this offering unto YeHoVaH. Approximately 1.5 hrs.

Feast of Firstfruits   1 DVD – $15.00

"Hear, O Israel" is a call for ALL of the People Of YeHoVaH to Hear and to Obey His Commands. Often times when people hear the word "Israel," they think "Jews." Israel consists of 12 Tribes; the Jews are only one of those tribes. In this eye-opening, engaging and life-changing teaching "Hear, O Israel," Arthur Bailey explains in-depth of Yeshua's response and the benefits of what it really means to Hear and to Obey! Approximately 2.5 hrs.

Hear, O Israel   2 DVDs – $25.00

In his dynamic, life-changing teaching: "How to Hear God's Voice," author and teacher Arthur Bailey shares important Biblical truths that will help you identify and distinguish the voice of the Almighty from all other voices. In this 4-DVD collection you will learn:

- Why YeHoVah communicates with his people
- Why he wants you to hear his voice
- How to identify his voice from others
- Where he most likely speaks to you

And so much more! Approximately 5.5 hrs.

How to Hear God's Voice   4 DVDs – $45.00

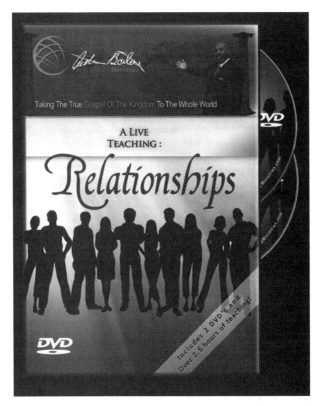

In this 2-DVD teaching series, Arthur Bailey presents from Scripture how the relationships in our lives must be categorized and prioritized according to their importance. You will learn:

- The kind of relationship the Almighty wants with you
- How to categorize and prioritize your relationships according to Scripture
- How to identify and rectify wrong relationships

And so much more! Approximately 2.5 hrs.

Relationships   2 DVDs – $25.00

Join Arthur Bailey as he explains the parable taught by Yeshua after having shared with His disciples about the Gospel of The Kingdom being preached to the whole world before the end comes. Yeshua gives a parable about three servants who were given specific talents. What distinguished the wise servant from the wicked servant in this parable was determined by what they did with the talents they had been given. Approximately 1.5 hrs.

Maximizing your Talents   1 DVD – $15.00

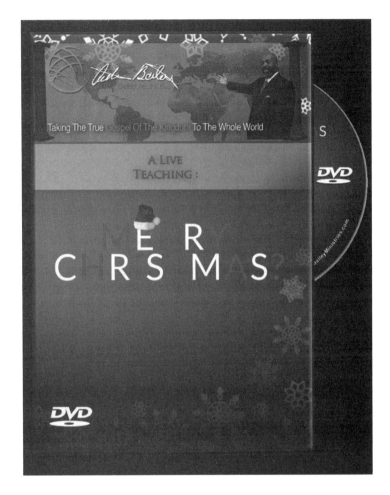

Where did Christmas originate? What does the Bible have to say about Christmas and its relationship to the birth of Christ? Is Christmas even in the Bible? Should Christ be in Christmas? Is Jesus the reason for the season? How should true believers respond to Christmas? These questions and so many more will be answered in this timeless Christmas Message, "MERRY CHRISTMAS?" Approx. 1.5 hrs.

Merry Christmas?   1 DVD – $15.00

The ReNEWed Covenant is 1.5 hours of teaching. In this teaching "The ReNEWed Covenant"; Arthur Bailey gives a clear, eye-opening, biblical explanation of what the New Covenant is, and with whom it is made. He explains how Jews and Gentiles enter into this covenant, and what it means for believers today. You will understand why it is called The ReNEWed Covenant, and the significant power that is released within the lives of all who embrace the ReNEWed Covenant. This Teaching Will Change Your Life Forever! Approximately 1.5 hrs.

The ReNEWed Covenant   1 DVD – $15.00

In this powerful 4-DVD teaching "The Power of The Holy Spirit," author and teacher Arthur Bailey reveals the pre-requisites all believers must meet to be filled with the Holy Spirit and Power. What is this power Yeshua spoke of? Is this power still available for the disciples of Yeshua today? How can the disciples of Yeshua operate in this power today? These and many other questions will be answered in this fascinating and informative teaching series. Approximately 5.5 hrs.

The Power of the Holy Spirit   4 DVDs – $45.00

In this teaching Arthur Bailey will address:
- What is Prosperity?   - Is Prosperity Biblical?
- Is Poverty a Curse?   - Can Believers be Prosperous?
- What does the Bible Teach about Prosperity?
- What is True Biblical Prosperity?

What you believe about prosperity will determine what you can and cannot receive from YeHovaH. This teaching series will leave you with a wealth of information. It will help you understand why YeHoVaH wants His people to be *prosperous*, and what *true Biblical prosperity* looks like! Approximately 5.5 hrs.

True Biblical Prosperity   4 DVDs – $45.00

The Church world has taken a conversation Yeshua had with a Pharisee at night, and built powerhouse ministries teaching a gospel message of salvation and altar calls. Many sermons have been taught about being born again and what it should mean to believers today. But what does *John 3:16* really teach us within the context it is written? Like many other Biblical passages, this much-quoted verse is taught and preached in a manner that has become isolated from the passage context in which it was originally written. Approximately 2.5 hrs.

You Must Be Born Again   2 DVDs – $25.00

Paul wrote in the book of Romans, *"But God commendeth his love toward us, in that, while we were yet sinners, Messiah died for us"*. God demonstrated His love for us by giving His only begotten Son to die for our sins. How can we show our love for God? In this 4-DVD teaching, Arthur Bailey will take you on a journey through the *greatest love story ever written*, and what our response to the love of God should be. It is more than just a story of salvation. It is a story of love; of overcoming, of victory, and of power. Approximately 5.5 hrs.

The Love of God   4 DVDs – $45.00

The Fall Feasts of YeHoVaH is a 6-DVD set with over 6.5 hours of teaching. This series include teachings on The Feast of Trumpets/Yom Teruah, Day of Atonement/Yom Kippur, The Feast of Tabernacles/Sukkot and The Last Great Day/Shemini Atzeret. The Introduction to the Fall Feasts will not only provide insight and understanding of the prophetic shadow pictures of good things to come; it will also help us understand how to celebrate these amazing days in a way that pleases Almighty YeHoVah.

The Fall Feast Of YeHoVaH   6 DVDs – $65.00

The DVDs listed in this book are just a sampling of the many teaching DVDs produced by Arthur Bailey Ministries. These teaching DVDs are packed with scriptural references; and are taught in a format that will encourage, strengthen, and enhance your spiritual journey to help you grow to maturity in Messiah Yeshua.

Visit   www.ArthurBaileyMinistries.com/Bookstore to order any of the DVDs listed here; or our online bookstore.

In addition to placing your order online on our secure website, you may also call in your order at 1-888-899-1479, or send your check or money order to:

Arthur Bailey Ministries
P.O. Box 49744
Charlotte, NC 28277